UNDERS

A JEW

by

H. L. ELLISON, B.D., B.A.

Author of

Men Spake from God. *Studies in the Prophets of the Old Testament.*

Ezekiel: The Man and his Message.

From Tragedy to Triumph. *The Message of the Book of Job.*

The Household Church.

The Centrality of the Messianic Idea for the Old Testament.

The Mystery of Israel.

THE OLIVE PRESS

Vincent House, Vincent Square, London SWIP 2PX

TO

Those who have given

A Life-Time of Service to

THE JEWISH PEOPLE OUT OF LOVE TO

THEIR JEWISH SAVIOUR

Reprinted 1973

Reprinted 1978

ISBN 0 904054 01 2

FOREWORD

THERE are somewhat less than half a million Jews in Great Britain. If we except about a tenth of them, who were not born in this country, most are hardly distinguishable as Jews to the untrained eye and ear, even though the predominant physical types among them are not typical for Britain. Though many of them are passionately interested in the welfare of the State of Israel, with only rare exceptions their first loyalty is to the land in which they live and of which they are proud to be citizens. When we meet them in local government, the professions and arts, in trade and industry, there is normally nothing that distinguishes them from us. The moment, however, that religion is mentioned there is a wall of separation. This is not the blank incomprehension of the average newcomer from India or Pakistan nor the radical rejection met with in the modern atheist and humanist. If we may illustrate by the trivial, it is more like that popular toy, the "tricky dogs", where the plastic animals mounted on magnets both attract and repel.

This little book has been written for convinced Christians. As such we presumably desire to share our knowledge of Jesus Christ with those who do not know Him, even though we may not be vitally concerned whether they accept our estimate of Him. It may be that we simply wish to understand those who share our belief in a creating and loving God without accepting that He has revealed Himself in His Son Jesus Christ. Whatever our attitude, we know that contacts with our fellow-men that exclude the possibility of contact on the spiritual level will never lead to a full understanding or real fellowship. This applies equally to our contacts with Jews.

For profitable conversation with them, as with others who come from a different tradition, we must have some idea of their position, preconceptions and prejudices. Irrespective of the terms used, of the immediate purpose and of the final outcome envisaged, intelligent conversation or dialogue—the modern vogue word—between Jews and Christians is becoming increasingly popular. This little book is intended to help this forward by describing, so far as seemed necessary, the Jew, his religion, his outlook on life and his misconceptions of Christianity as objectively as possible. There are numerous books by Jews—some are mentioned in the Bibliography—that cover most of the ground far more effectively, but they do not take Christian preconceptions and prejudices sufficiently into account. Equally there are a number of outstanding works by Christians on the subject, but they tend to be too extensive or too detailed and specialized for the ordinary parish minister or Christian layman who happens to meet Jews in the ordinary course of his daily life.

Ideally a similar book should be written about the Christian for Jewish readers and I should be the first to rejoice when this comes to pass.

Should this book fall into the hands of a Jewish reader, I would ask him to remember that what the Gentile Christian finds hard to understand and wants to know is not always that which looms largest in Jewish thought. Interpretation can never be a purely photographic process.

By sheer accident the major part of the work on this book was done in the heart of India with probably no Jew within four hundred miles of me and the only link with the continuing life of Jewry the weekly arrival of the London *Jewish Chronicle*. I trust that this separation from the Jewish scene may have created a greater objectivity and concentration on the essentials.

CONTENTS

Chapter I

WHO IS A JEW?

THE question of who is a Jew is the subject of serious discussion by Jewish religious leaders and Israeli lawyers, but the problems they are trying to solve are never likely to become the concern of the readers of this book. While the visitor to Israel may well be amazed at the variety of physical types displayed by the Jews there, their acceptance as Jews is based in over 99% of the cases on birth. Similarly in Britain, those whom we meet who are willing to identify themselves as Jews (apart from a very rare proselyte) have in common mostly that they were born of Jewish parents—in fact a Jewish mother is sufficient—and that they have some valid reason for affirming Jewishness.

The modern Jew, if we may ignore his biological inheritance, is the product of the interplay of various factors, the importance of which varies from family to family and individual to individual. The most important are traditional religion, traditional culture, which has not been uniform throughout Jewry, general Western culture and thought and the reaction to Christian and Islamic propaganda and persecution. There was a time when Islam had a greater influence on the Jew for good and bad than Christianity, but since those directly moulded by it are seldom met in Britain, it may be ignored.

This interplay of influences is capable of creating an incredible number of combinations from the ultra-orthodox Jew living solely for religion in the same way as some of his ancestors in the Middle Ages to the ultra-modern man immersed in technology and living by Marxist or existentialist philosophy. This means that to speak and think of *the* Jew is the infallible way to misinterpret the individual we may happen to meet. All we can do is to examine the main formative influences in the hope that we may grasp what makes the individual a Jew and so understand him better.

We must, in addition, avoid that incredible Nazi error which proclaimed that Jewishness was purely a matter of birth, of biology. Some of the worst sufferers in Germany were those who discovered for the first time that they had a Jewish grandparent, or even it might be a Jewish parent, when they had to delve into their ancestry in order to prove that they were pure Aryans and so keep their positions. In any real sense, except for racial bigots and madmen, there was nothing really Jewish about them, even though they might have satisfied the definition of Jew for Israel's Law of the Return.

The typical Israeli would tell one that a Jew is anyone who feels himself to be a Jew. The orthodox, however, insist that to be a Jew by birth one must have a Jewish mother. Behind this ruling there lie probably the events of Ezr. 9. 10. However this may have worked in the past, the ruling has created many anomalies in our modern world. Ben Gurion, the first Prime Minister of Israel, remarked that while his granddaughter was a Gentile—she had to join the Synagogue as a proselyte before she could marry—Kruschev's was a Jewess, for his son had married a religionless Jewess, while Ben Gurion's had married an English woman. To complicate matters the Supreme Court has ruled that a Jew who has become a Christian is not to be regarded as a Jew for the purposes of the Law of the Return, even though the rabbis regard him as one. In addition there is a small group of people on the fringe of Jewry for whom acceptance religiously is so difficult, that they almost always go lost to it. The bastard or ***mamzer***, a child born in adultery or incest, is excluded from the community by Deut. 23:2. For our purposes we shall regard the man who is willing to be known as a Jew to be one and shall ignore those who may be considered Jews by accident of birth.

Chapter II

ORTHODOX JUDAISM

IN Western Europe, down to the time of the French Revolution, to be a Jew was virtually equivalent to holding the traditional practices and beliefs of the rabbis,[1] which so far as practices were concerned had received an apparently final definition in the *Shulchan Aruch* (1565). Indeed we sometimes find the strictly conformist Jew called a Shulchan Aruch Jew. It is, however, essential to realize that the more strictly conformist a Jew is the less likely he is to use the word 'orthodox'. It was borrowed from Christianity in the 19th century with the rise of 'Liberal Judaism', and is today increasingly being replaced by terms like Torah-observant. The fact is that while there are certain basic theological beliefs without which a Jew, in the old sense, is inconceivable, the Synagogue normally enquires only about a man's behaviour. Where this is satisfactory, the correctness of his beliefs is taken for granted and no questions are asked about them. So H. M. Loewe has suggested the use of orthopraxy rather than orthodoxy; though the term has not gained wide vogue, it is certainly preferable.

The French Revolution breached the bastions of tradition in the West. In the east of Europe these were eroded by the Haskalah (Enlightenment), Marxist Socialism and Zionism, but it was not until after the 1914 war that traditionalism was in full retreat; it was almost wiped out by the Nazi holocaust. During the present century modern secular thought and life has left few Jews in Europe and America uninfluenced, so that traditionalism today is normally relative rather than absolute. This is particularly the case in America.

The centuries' long identification of Jewish nationality and religion has made the Jew take for granted that the same identification of Gentile and Christian is equally legitimate. Often one of the first surprises for the Jew, when he begins a serious conversation with a true Christian, is to find that the latter condemns the behaviour of the irreligious Gentile neigh-

[1] This may be seen in the furore caused when Spinoza (1632-1677) left the Synagogue without becoming a Christian.

bour as much as does the Jew and denies his right to be called a Christian. The Pauline distinction between the Jew, the Gentile and the Church of God (1 Cor. 10:32) is one that few Jews have grasped.

Because of the age-old sway of 'orthodox' Judaism, many Jews without religion think of it as the norm to which they would have to return, were they to regain faith in God, and many who call themselves 'liberal' or 'reform' Jews—the former is the usual British term, the latter the American—have a barely hidden guilty conscience when they compare their practice with that of their ancestors. Hence most Jews, when they look critically at Christianity, tend to take traditional Judaism as the pattern to judge it by. It is most important to realize this. There are many Jews who profess to have completely abandoned Judaism, yet they use its concepts to motivate their rejection of Christianity. In other words, anyone wishing to speak positively about Christianity to a Jew should know something of the basic tenets of Judaism.

The only more widely known Jewish creed is the Thirteen Principles of Faith by Maimonides (1135-1204); these may be found in any standard prayer-book (*siddur*). They are not recited at any service, nor are they binding on the man who conforms to traditional practice. It should never be taken for granted that they are accepted, though the greater the degree of orthopraxy the greater the probability that this is so. In the lack of a binding creed one can offer only those points where there is virtual unanimity, viz:

A. There is only one God, uniquely one and indivisible.

B. This God chose Israel to be His people in a special way and sealed the election by an eternal covenant.

C. The choice of Israel involved Israel's acceptance of God's Torah (Law), so that the two are now and always inseparably linked.

D. God's purpose is the establishment of His universal rule upon earth.

In our treatment of these points we shall ignore those aspects where there is no real difference between Jewish and Christian theology. It may be well to add that the popular dictum that the Synagogue has no theology has done much harm. On points like the above-mentioned Jewish religious thinking is quite clear, even if it has never been developed as has been the case in the Church.

Chapter III

THE UNIQUENESS AND UNITY OF GOD

THE lasting effect of the Babylonian exile was to etch in the Jews' hearts an abiding hatred of idolatry—those who did not share it were soon lost among their heathen neighbours. This led increasingly to a denial of the possibility of any other Divine being. The great prophets had preached an ethical monotheism, i.e. the existence of other gods could be ignored; now the stress was on their non-existence. A Jew may believe in the existence of supernatural beings both good and evil, in angels, demons, etc., and in some circles even in links between God and man, e.g. Philo's *logos* (Word), which played no part in the development of Judaism, the earlier rabbinic *memra* (Word), which was increasingly ignored owing to Christian pressures, and the mystic *sephirot* or Divine emanations, which play such a part in the Kabbalah, but they are all part of God's creation, however much they may be higher than man.

Later, in reaction against Christian Trinitarian teaching and under the influence of Muslim thought and Aristotelian philosophy, for *many* God came to be regarded as the essentially unknowable. He has revealed His will and character by His acts, but no human attribute may be affirmed of Him. Even where His revelation of Himself uses human terms, these may never be understood from a strictly human standpoint. Indeed, even His unity was seen as being more than human. If the Christian stressed the mystery of the Divine trinity, the Jewish thinker underlined the ineffable mystery of the Divine unity, 'like no other unity'.

While in New Testament times the cross was the great stumbling block in the way of a Jew's acceptance of Jesus of Nazareth as the Messiah, with the development of the Church's Christology this shifted to the Incarnation. For the traditional Jew it is impossible that God should have become man in any real sense of the word.

Probably most Jews still believe that Christians worship

two, if not three, Gods—are they always that far wrong? Those brought up in predominantly Roman Catholic or Orthodox countries often assume that the third person of the Trinity is the Virgin Mary. It is true that the small but increasing section of Jewry really interested in Christianity realizes that Trinitarianism is strictly monotheistic, though it is not understood. But even for them the doctrine that God should in any sense have become man is completely unacceptable, even as the Sonship of Christ is to the Muslim.

"Our God contracted to a span
Incomprehensibly made man"

as Charles Wesley sang in his Christmas hymn is for them sheer blasphemy.

It should also be borne in mind that for a religious Jew the use of images and pictures as well as of a crucifix is a major breach of the second commandment, even if they are not used directly in worship. His objection to a plain cross is that it symbolizes for him persecution over the centuries in the name of a crucified Jesus, in which the persecutors all too often carried a cross in their hands. It goes so far that many will not use a plus sign, but write ⊥ instead of +. Whatever we many think of the use of the sign of the cross in baptism, it is best omitted in the case of a convert from Judaism. It is a common vulgar superstition that the baptized Jew has somehow had a cross branded or tattooed on him.

Chapter IV

GOD'S CHOICE OF ISRAEL

MANY of those who dislike the Jews justify themselves by pointing to their attitude of superiority, which they attribute to the Jewish sense of election. Where this attitude of superiority really exists, its cause is another. So very often the moral standards of the religious Jew have tended to be superior to those of many of his Gentile neighbours. One of the main obstacles to the presentation of Christ to the Jew has been and is that the Christianity he has observed and experienced is so often inferior to the Judaism he has been reared in. The sense of jealousy mentioned by Paul (Rom. 11:11, 14) is awakened only by contact with the truly Spirit-filled Christian.

However strong a Jew's sense of election, it does not normally give him any sense of superiority over the Gentile. The sages of Israel fully assimilated the teaching of passages like Deut. 7:7; 9:4, 6; 10:22. They were quite clear that God had chosen them in loving grace, cf. Deut. 4:37; 7:8. There were and are differences of opinion as to why God chose Israel, but the sufferings of Jewry down the centuries made it impossible for the normal Jew to feel conceited because of his election. Indeed there have sometimes been those who wished in the bitterness of their sufferings that the election had never taken place. A Jew may believe that the Patriarchs, Moses and other outstanding figures in Israel's history acquired merit from which he can profit—he may even believe that this is true of some outstandingly righteous men of his own time—but he acknowledges, especially on the Day of Atonement, that Israel existed and exists by virtue of God' grace and love.

We should accept the fact that for the religious Jew God's election is as great a reality as for the most fervent Calvinist, even though it is national rather than personal and its outworking is this-worldly and existential rather than soteriological. The very fact that it is not personal makes it less dependent on feelings. So strong is the concept that even the materialist and atheist in Jewry find it hard to free themselves from it. One of the most potent influences in awakening this feeling in the young and keeping it alive in later years is the annual celebration of the Passover, which, together with that of the Day of Atonement, is the last vestige of religion to be abandoned when all else has gone.

Because of this concept of election religious Jewry cannot recognize a division between 'church' and state. Israel today is officially a secular state, but the strictly orthodox within it claim that Jewish citizens—nearly a fifth are not Jews—should conform to the rabbinic law as well as to that of the state, and that the latter should not conflict with the former. Though the laxer and non-religious majority resist this, in those areas susceptible to easy public control the orthodox have been remarkably successful in getting their own way. Since the Jew, as was said earlier, normally equates Gentile and Christian, the Church's frequent withdrawal from public affairs is a major stumbling-block to him. Especially today he finds it almost impossible to understand or condone the Christian's frequent silence about anti-Jewish or other racialist manifestations, and above all almost complete failure of the German churches in the Nazi period.

Equally, traditional Judaism cannot find any place for the voluntary principle and denominationalism. Local practice (*minhag*) has always been recognized. But while the sermon, if there is one, will be in the vernacular, throughout traditional Jewry the synagogue service and private daily prayer is always in Hebrew, with an occasional Aramaic prayer; local variations are so small as to be virtually unrecognizable for the uninitiated. True, there are some striking differences in some pure externals in the behaviour of different groups, but few of them go beneath the surface.

For the traditional Jew there is nothing objectionable in the refusal of most orthodox rabbis to recognize liberal and reform rabbis and services, and he normally approves of the position in Israel, where such rabbis however great their learning, have no recognized status, and where their services, with few exceptions, are held only under difficulties. On the other hand, these liberal Jews are welcomed to most traditionalist synagogues without any question, for the fact of their being Jews overrides their views and even their untraditional practices.

This means that while a Jew can understand the division between the Catholic and the Protestant, or between the traditionalist Christian and the modernist, he finds the further cleavages a stumbling-block, especially when they create very real barriers between Christian and Christian, which virtually deny the Church's claim to be God's elect people. It is interesting that a certain type of Jew is probably more interested in the existence and activity of the World Council of Churches than are many Christians. We may express this in another way. However much the traditional Synagogue might like to restrict the term Jew to its own members, it knows it cannot, because man's judgment is overruled by God's election. When a church seeks to define the term Christian in the light of its theology, practice and membership, it subordinates God's election to man's judgment.

From an early date the Church ignored Paul's teaching in Rom. 9-11, cf. especially 9:3-5; 11:1, 2, 28, 29, and declared that the election of Israel as a nation had become null and void, and that its privileges had been transferred to the Church, the 'true', or 'spiritual' Israel. Many a Jew who has been attracted to Jesus Christ has been repelled by the Church's claim, for he knew that he could not deny God's lasting election of the people to which he belonged. Today we have a revolt against this false concept in the Hebrew-Christian movement, which is a little over a century old. Its members are all associated with a variety of Christian churches; their theology is orthodox; but they insist that they are conscious of a double election as Jews and as Christians. They have no feeling of superiority over their non-Jewish fellow church-members, but they are conscious of a double duty to God. It has happened that the knowledge that such a movement can exist within the Church has been decisive in determining some Jews' attitude to Jesus Christ.

Chapter V

THE LAW OF MOSES

HISTORICALLY the great turning point in the religious history of Israel came with Ezra's reading of the Law in Jerusalem (Neh. 8). This was the beginning of what we may legitimately call Judaism, though in one sense it began only with the destruction of the Temple in A.D.70. It is a matter of controversy how far back Ezra's attitude towards the Law can be traced, but there is agreement between Jewish and Christian scholars that it was through his influence that the Law became the normative and formative principle in Jewish existence.

It takes no profound study of the legal portions of the Pentateuch to realize that in spite of their detail they are far from covering the whole of life and its possibilities. A situation like that pictured in 1 Sam. 30:24, 25 shows that in an earlier period of Israel's history legislation without any appeal to earlier precedents was considered right and proper provided the underlying motivation was reasonable. The principles introduced, or established by Ezra were:—

(i) The Torah was not merely basic to the Sinai covenant but also one of its main motivations;

(ii) It was the concern of each individual and not merely of the authorities, civil and religious;

(iii) In principle it covered the whole of life.

Those whom we know as the scribes[1]—a title borne by Ezra himself (Ezr.7:6)—took the meaning of *torah,* i.e. instruction, not law, seriously. They accepted that from the commandments that had been given and their motivation, especially in Deuteronomy, one could infer principles and guidelines for legislation on matters not mentioned and for adapting the commandments to changing social circumstances. Gradually they tried on the one hand to codify the laws that were already there, and on the other to legislate for every situation in life. In this process they had three main motives.

[1] *Sopherim*—they did copy the sacred books, but only because they first knew them, often by heart, and so could avoid errors.

They wished to discover God's will exactly, to protect those who might transgress it in ignorance, and to close any loopholes that might be found by those who approached the Torah purely legalistically.

Since these principles and the legislation deduced from them were increasingly recognized as valid and were virtually accepted among Jews by A.D. 150, the traditional Jew understands far more under *Torat Mosheh* (the Law of Moses) than does the Christian. He means not merely the Pentateuch, the *torah she-biktav* (the Written Law), but also the *torah she-be'al-peh* (the Oral Law), which has for him equal authority; indeed Torah for him means both. He expresses it by saying that Moses received the (Oral) Law on Mt. Sinai and passed it on to Joshua, who passed it on to the prophets, etc. Various passages in the Talmud make it clear that this is not to be taken literally, though it is so understood by many pious Jews, but that the correct principles of interpreting the Torah were imparted with it. We might say that the rabbinic claim was that the same spirit that was operative in the prophets, regarded above all as interpreters of the Torah, was operative in the concensus of the rabbis. Rabbi L. Rabinowitz, speaking to a group of Christian workers in Israel in 1963, expressed it by saying 'It is not entirely correct to say that Orthdox Judaism believes in the Bible. It believes in the Bible as interpreted and explained by the rabbis'. This, incidentally, has close contacts with the Catholic concept of tradition.

It was decided that there are 613 commandments or precepts in the Torah, 248 of them being affirmative and 365 negative. To guarantee that these were kept a 'fence' was made about them, i.e. further laws were evolved, which though not clearly involved in the original 613 would guarantee that they were kept by the ignorant and careless. In addition other laws were deduced for matters left undealt with in the Pentateuch. By A.D. 200 all the main fields of life had been covered and the laws were codified in the Mishnah. These were further discussed and amplified in the Gemara, finished about A.D. 500[2]. Though in one sense this was final, in another the

[2] Mishnah and Gemara together form the Talmud, which, however, is far from being merely a collection of laws. It gives us a unique insight into Rabbinic thought, beliefs sacred and profane, and methods of Scriptural interpretation. The sections linked with the earliest rabbis mentioned by name throw a flood of light on the Jewish background to the New Testament.

ever-changing pattern of life found the rabbis capable of adapting the legislation to new situations, until today they can legislate on problems like the use of electric current for a microphone or refrigerator on the Sabbath, or the validity of tinned meat or a television set. This creates no problem for the observant Jew. His own knowledge may well be limited, but his queries will be answered by the rabbi, who is conceived of as an expert on the Law, not as a priest, a leader of congregational worship, a preacher or teacher, even though he may carry out some of these functions.

The Christian is in danger of numerous misunderstandings when he thinks of the rabbinic concept of Torah. However arbitrary some of the rabbinic laws may seem to the modern man, for the pious Jew the whole is an expression of God's grace and character. It is His greatest gift to Israel, and the election of Israel is bound up with the Torah.

While there is a reward for the keeping of the Torah—it is only a hyper-spiritualized form of Christianity that has no place for rewards—the teaching of the rabbis is that only the keeping of its precepts for its own sake and with devotedness of heart is really acceptable to God. While there are legalistic Jews, as there are Christians, it is hardly fair to call traditional Judaism at its best purely legalistic. If one grants its basic concept, viz. that God has given a law which it is a man's duty and privilege to keep, the detailed working out of the commandments is for the most part logical.

For someone brought up in and continuing to live in strictly observant circles the observance of the minutiae of the Torah becomes relatively easy and automatic. The difficulties come for the Jew exposed to the pressure of a society which ignores or is hostile to the Torah. In estimating Peter's judgment (Acts 15:10) we must not forget that he came from Galilee, where Gentile influence was strong. These difficulties have, however, always been mitigated by the Rabbinic principle based on Lev. 18:5, Deut. 4:1, etc., cf. Rom. 7:10, that since the Torah had been given that man might have life through it, its commandments might be eased or even broken, where danger to life was involved. In the case of a genuine threat to life any commandment might be broken except three, viz. the prohibitions of idolatry, murder and adultery. In these cases the Jew had rather 'to sanctify the Name' by laying down his life. It should not be forgotten that the pious Jew regards the acceptance of baptism as an act of idolatry as well as of apostasy, for it involves the acceptance of Jesus as another God.

As a result of this principle very much of what passes as orthodoxy in Western society today represents more or less compromise. The strictly observant Jew, unless he is very wealthy and so can create his own environment, is likely to be confined to small pockets in the big cities, e.g. Stamford Hill in London, Gateshead, and Williamsburg in New York. Even in Israel it is possible to observe the Torah in its full strictness only by withdrawing from certain aspects of national life, and those who wish to do it are generally found in certain well-defined areas, e.g. Mea Shearim in Jerusalem and Bne Beraq near Tel-Aviv. Hence, if a Jew claims to be orthodox, all that can be taken for granted is his acceptance in theory of the primacy of the Torah and of the traditional rabbinic interpretation of it.

He does not understand the traditional Christian division of the Law into legal, moral and ceremonial, and the Christian claim of freedom from law awakens no welcoming echo from him. The greatness of Torah for him lies just in its embracing every aspect of life; he seeks freedom within the Law by perfectly conforming to it. If he feels dissatisfaction, it will rather be because he finds himself excluded by it from much that modern life has to offer. If he knows his tradition, he will agree that portions of the Torah will vanish in the days of the Messiah and the age to come, because they will no longer be needed, but he cannot conceive of its being superceded even by the Messiah, one of whose functions is to make its perfect observance possible.

Before a Christian can hope for profitable dialogue with a religious Jew he must first clarify his own thinking about the relationship of Law and Grace and also of the Christian's to the Law of Moses. It is a commonplace for the educated Jew to accept Jesus, as he understands Him, and to reject Paul as a rejector of the Torah. He affirms that Jesus did in fact keep the Law and never envisaged its rejection.

To say that the average Christian has little understanding of Pauline teaching on the Law is merely to state the obvious. This is obvious not merely in the insistence on the sanctity of the Ten Commandments by virtually all Christians but also in the wide range of rules and regulations which are enforced in the various denominations. It is virtually impossible for a Jew to take the normal Christian attitude to the Law seriously; it seems to him merely an effort to avoid the "yoke" of the Law. It should not be forgotten that the Synagogue has virtually no theology of the Holy Spirit and hence has no understanding for the true Christian teaching on the subject.

Chapter VI

GOD'S PURPOSE FOR THE WORLD

THE concept of the Day of the Lord is as central for the Old Testament as is that of the return of Christ for the New, even though it is not so frequently mentioned. It looked forward to the day when the earth would be full of the knowledge of the Lord, and men would not hurt or destroy in all His holy mountain, i.e. the earth. By the time of Christ this concept had become inseparably linked with the person of the Messiah, but the Christian stress on Jesus as the Messiah has always tended to confuse the average Jew. For this there are two main reasons. The Christian concept of the Messiah has always differed from that of the Jews, and the Jewish concept has been greatly modified by repeated disappointments.

The main stress laid by the Christian on the Messiah has probably always been on Him as the Suffering Servant and on His saving work for the individual. Ever since the break-down of the mediaeval Catholic concept of the state Jesus' role as world-king is more often than not relegated to the future, and in practice minimized. But even Qumran, though it took the picture of the Servant's vicarious sufferings seriously, does not seem to have reached a full Messianic interpretation. The Synagogue's attitude towards the prophecy has always been uncertain, and it has always been relegated to the background. At the same time, if the application of it to Israel is now standard, it is because of the way Christian apologists used it in disputations in which the Jews were forced to take part. It is not found until the time of Rashi.[1] Repeatedly there has been in certain Jewish circles a tendency to regard the Messiah as a super-man, but he has never been looked on as more than a man.

For the Jew the Messiah is the deliverer, but the deliverer

[1] Rashi, i.e. Rabbi Solomon Yitzchaki (1040-1105), lived in France and was one of the greater mediaeval commentators on Scripture and Talmud alike.

from outside pressures, not from inner ones, i.e. sins. It was quite Jewish, when many of the Yemenites, after having been brought to Israel in 1948, regarded Ben Gurion as at least a Messianic figure. True enough, the Messiah is often enough linked with deliverance from sin, but it is from sin due to the pressure of outside forces. It is a rabbinic conviction that most Jews placed in ideal surroundings would keep the Law perfectly. The Messiah will deal with those that do not, either by judgment or kindly pressure. The Messiah is not a new lawgiver but the enforcer of the Torah.

Sholem Asch pointed out that the demand by some of the scribes, Pharisees, Sadducees and people in general for a sign (Matt. 12:48; 16:1, Mk. 8:11, Lk. 11:16, 29, Jn. 2:18; 6:30) was entirely justified from their point of view.[2] Moses had demonstrated his God-given authority by showing signs (Exod. 4:1-10, 27-30), and except for the rare mystic with esoteric teaching the rabbis have always based themselves on the authority of Moses. Jesus' contemporaries were not denying that He might possibly possess an authority that did not go back to Moses, as indeed He implied by His 'but I say unto you', but they considered that if this were the case, He should justify His claims by signs greater than those done by Moses. This was the supreme evidential importance of the resurrection, at least so far as the Jews were concerned. This is a subject that the modern Jew normally tries to avoid, cf. the strangely weak conclusion to *The Nazarene* by Sholem Asch and that strange work *The Passover Plot* by H. Schonfield.

It is not merely that the work of Jesus as the Messiah does not conform to the traditional Jewish concept; seen in the light of the latter He has not done the Messiah's work at all. A modern, well-educated, travelled Jew, who has had wide contacts with Christians, especially with those who are Christians in life as well as creed, will have a deep respect for Jesus of Nazareth. Provided he knows that his confessions will not be used as a debating point against him, he will readily acknowledge that Jesus has proved to be a transforming power among the heathen nations, and that the rabbis could never have done the missionary work that Christ's followers have done. He may even go so far as to say that the heathen had to have Jesus, and that in that sense He may be called the Messiah of the Gentiles—but He is not the Messiah of the Jews, because

[2] *My Personal Faith*, pp. 109f.

the Jews do not need what He has done for the Gentiles, while He has not done the Jewish Messiah's work.

This may be illustrated and explained by the story told of a famous rabbi in Europe. When a Christian visitor was urging the claims of Jesus as Messiah, he went over to the window, looked out on the busy city street for a few minutes, returned to his chair and said sadly, "I should like to believe you, but nothing has changed; the Messiah has not come." This is a graphic way of saying that for the Jew the Messiah is the transformer of this world order, or the one who ushers in this transformation. For him the Christian's stress on the Second Coming is a mere dodging of the issue.

It needs to be added that the same process of rationalization may be seen on both sides. There are many Christians who have reduced the expected Parousia to a gradual transformation of mankind and of the world through the spiritual influence of the exalted Christ. Similarly, there are many religious Jews—possibly the majority—for whom the Messiah is merely a personification of the Messianic hope. Ever since the last and probably greatest Messianic disappointment linked with Shabbethai Zevi (1626-1676) it would seem that the majority of Jews have ceased to expect a personal Messiah without losing the hope of a Messianic age. Certainly this is true today, though the hope of a personal Messiah may often be found in the most unexpected quarters. So to say to a Jew, "I have found the Messiah", will seldom create the thrill of hope and expectation it once did.

There is, however, another factor in the Jewish outlook on the future to be considered. Even the antisemite will sometimes grudgingly acknowledge the generosity of the Jewish philanthropist, not merely to his own community, but also to the community at large, even if the blackest motivation may then be ascribed to it. It is very difficult to know what the average Jew believes about life after death. In theory the orthodox accept the resurrection of the dead for a life on a new and transformed earth, and the liberals a continuing spiritual existence. In practice the attitude of many of them in the face of death suggests that it is theory and longing rather than reality; in fact almost all live as though this were the only life to be lived. The Jew normally sympathizes with the sceptic who claims that Christianity looks for "pie in the sky bye and bye". He considers that it is this world that holds the hope for the future, and he must help in its transformation, even if it will be finally brought about by God's breaking into history once again. That is one reason why the stress on the transformation of the soil in Israel need not be a sign of national pride or a rationalizing of Zionist claims.

It is this positive attitude to this material world and its material problems that goes far to explain Jewry's alleged major contribution to world socialism in general and to Communism in particular. Though this has been greatly exaggerated, especially as regards the latter, there is considerable truth in it. It is hard for the Jew, religious or secular, to accept the *status quo,* and in most countries the average Jew has seen in the parties of the left the only hope for the removal of social wrongs.

The Jew recognizes the existence of Christian philanthropy and often supports it, where it is not exclusively Christian in its scope of purpose. He is also normally prepared to cooperate with Christian social movements which are for the general good of the community. But he is apt to note with dismay that the churches as a whole tend to have a theoretical rather than a positive attitude towards the major social problems and injustices—he has the same sceptical attitude towards episcopal and ministerial pronouncements as he has towards those of his own rabbis.

One cannot expect many Jews to realize that it is exactly in this field that some of the most agonizing reappraisals in Christian theology and ethical thought are taking place. He is far more conscious that most of his sufferings since the time of the emperor Constantine have been inflicted by Christians. In addition, though he does not blame the churches for the Nazi persecutions and the holocaust, he is painfully and often bitterly aware that in this period it was not only in Germany that the churches failed to deal with antisemitism among their members. He knows too that today they are largely indifferent to the persecution in Russia of the Jews in particular and of religion in general. He cannot understand in addition how the churches in general, in contrast to smaller groups within them, fail to reach a decision in principle on the State of Israel and so often betray a pro-Arab bias. This is not the expression of a partisan view by the writer; it may easily be seen by studying numerous W.C.C. and National Council of Churches statements. Particularly resented is the failure of the Vatican State officially to recognize the existence of the State of Israel.

So the Jew is apt to say that not only did Jesus not bring about a social transformation, but what transformation there has been has very often been the fruit of secular movements in the teeth of opposition from the Roman Catholic and other established churches. Moreover he considers the average Christian's lack of interest in social transformation to be a sign of his not taking the subject very seriously. It is not a question here of the validity or otherwise of Jewish opinion; it is the opinion of a vast majority of those Jews who are sufficiently interested in Jesus to take an intelligent interest in the Church.

Chapter VII

THE LIBERAL JEW

ONE effect of the Napoleonic emancipation of the Jews was the Reform movement, which began among Jews in Germany. Emancipation implied that Jews were to be regarded as full citizens in a state in which religion or the lack if it, was a personal matter. Many Jews considered that it involved them in the obligation to approximate to their fellow-citizens as closely as loyalty to their religion would permit.

Reform Judaism in its inception was an attempt to adapt the synagogue service to the new conditions. Organs were introduced,[1] the prayers shortened, some of them being in German, a regular sermon was preached, etc. While such changes may seem of small importance to the modern Christian, those familiar with British Church history may remember the furore created in some circles by the introduction of hymns instead of metrical psalms and paraphrases, of organs instead of the precentor's pitch-pipe, and above all of liturgies and vestments. For the rabbinic Jew the changes were a denial of the divine origin and authority of the oral Torah, as indeed the leaders of Reform realized clearly.

There are in Britain a few Reform Synagogues in this sense. They have never had over much influence, presumably because they came to be regarded as rather meaningless compromises. When Reform Judaism was transferred to the United States it found very little traditional Judaism to hold it back—indeed, since most of the Jewish communities at that time were small and scattered, traditional Judaism had become virtually an impossibility. So Reform developed and flourished in ways its founders could hardly have dreamt of, until in its extremer forms of worship the old pattern may be scarcely recognizable. When the great influx of East-European Jews came to

[1] The chief reasons for forbidding organs by the Orthodox were: (a) it is forbidden to play an organ on the Sabbath or a festival; (b) it is copying Gentile worship; (c) it is unseemly to rejoice in this way, while the Temple lies in ruins.

America after 1880, a high proportion of its leaders were socialists uninterested in religion, and so a traditionalist reaction to Reform was slow in building up.

In Britain the Liberal Jewish movement was founded by C. J. Montefiore (1859-1939), his chief helpers being Israel Abrahams and the Hon. Lily Montague. The term Liberal was used in preference to Reform, partly to avoid confusion with the already existing Reform synagogues, partly because its founders were conscious that they were aiming at more than mere reform. If one remembers that Reform synagogues in America and Liberal synagogues in Britain — in other parts of the world the designation will depend on the tradition in which their founders stood—have no fixed pattern of religious behaviour and worship, they may be regarded as two manifestations of the same spirit which have repeatedly interacted on one another. For convenience I shall restrict myself to the term Liberal, because it expresses the spirit of the movement better.

The Liberal Synagogue can be understood only against the background of Orthodoxy, just as historic Protestantism must be seen against that of the Church of Rome. It maintains that "the externals of Judaism may be altered to strengthen its internals"; the degree of alteration will depend on the individual synagogue. The point of real importance is that it denies the authority of rabbinic tradition and interpretation, even though they may be voluntarily retained in large measure for spiritual, national or sentimental reasons. Even more important is its acceptance, explicit or implicit, of the prophets as superior in spiritual importance to the Torah. Generally speaking they would accept a moderate higher critical assessment of the Old Testament.

With this shift of emphasis, while hostility to the Christian Church as manifested in history is largely maintained, a genuine effort is very often made to bring Jesus into their religious heritage. Indeed the difference between a Liberal synagogue and an Unitarian church is often one of emphasis.

Just because Liberal Judaism has no Talmud, no authoritative book of rules and doctrine, it is impossible to delineate it more closely. It is, however, safe to say that the four basic concepts of Orthodoxy, already dealt with, live on in Liberalism, though in modified forms.

While the Oral Torah is stripped of its authority and is

regarded solely as the wisdom of the past to be understood against the background of the past,[2] the primacy of the written Torah is maintained, only that now it is ethical principles alone that are stressed, and these are interpreted in the light of the prophetic message and the writings of the wise.

The Liberal doctrine of God is as monotheistic and anti-Trinitarian as the Orthodox, but its interpretation of Scriptural statements about God tends to be more humanistic and rationalistic than that of the traditionalist. It is just as strongly opposed to any realistic doctrine of the Incarnation, and is possibly even more sceptical of the possibility of Jesus' bodily resurrection, because it only takes the possibility of the continuation of spiritual existence seriously.

The election of Israel is accepted, but in a purely spiritual sense. The Jew is there to bring the true knowledge of God and of His will to mankind. Nationality and a homeland are of importance only if they further this spreading of the knowledge of God. Hence the dispersal of Jewry is normally regarded as necessary to Israel's mission, and Zionism is opposed, even if the existence of the State of Israel is recognized as a social necessity, at least for the time being. Since the Six-Day War, however, especially in America, an emotional attitude towards the State has grown up, which largely contradicts and sometimes overrules the spiritual and intellectual judgment of the Liberal.

The Liberal's influence is not to be measured by his numbers. His impact on the traditionalist in the United States has been so great as to create a new type of synagogue. The Conservative Synagogue may outwardly seem very like the Reform Synagogue in Britain; its modifications of the traditional services and customs do not normally go further, indeed often not so far, but in spirit it shows the triumph of Liberalism. While it will often be indignantly denied, the average member of the United Synagogue in Britain—the largest, richest and most influential synagogue body—would feel completely at home in a Conservative synagogue in America. In the much smaller Jewish community in Britain the influence of traditionalism has prevented an open ex-

[2] C. Montefiore and H. Loewe, *A Rabbinic Anthology,* is an outstanding example of Liberal sympathetic treatment of rabbinic thought; H. Loewe's share in the work was to provide an Orthodox balance through notes.

pression of liberalism by many who have in fact been won by its spirit.

It would be easy to mention the names of prominent Jewish intellectuals, especially in Israel, who in the expression of their views show every sign of belonging to the liberal camp, yet who honestly and sincerely claim to be orthodox. Because in their worship and daily behaviour they conform to traditional practice, they are reckoned to be orthodox, even by strict rabbis, yet clearly they are spiritually and intellectually liberals. This is one of the reasons why one must abandon the concept of 'the Jew' and learn to discover where the individual really stands.

An example of the modern Jew's refusal to fit neatly into categories may be seen in Rabbi Louis Jacobs. The former Chief-Rabbi Brodie refused to recognize his standing as a rabbi in the United Synagogue because of his views on the Torah. In speech and writing he had made it clear that he did not believe that even in its written form, still less in its oral one, had it all been given at Sinai, though he accepted its authority. Because he carries out its requirements he is indubitably orthodox and as such is the rabbi of the orthodox but independent New London Synagogue.

A practical outcome of Liberalism is that its rabbis have had a thoroughly modern education, however much they are acquainted with rabbinic tradition, and this is reflected in their preaching. The orthodox rabbi has almost inevitably concentrated on the past, and the more truly orthodox he is the more likely this is to be true. This in turn is reflected in his teaching and preaching. As a result, in dialogue between the Church and the Synagogue—in contradistinction to co-operation in good works—it is normally the Liberal rabbi who will be glad to participate. Even if the Orthodox rabbi is prepared to involve himself personally—the more genuinely orthodox, i.e. traditional, the less likely he is to do it—he will almost always object to the members of his synagogue being involved. This is for the perfectly adequate reason that he is fully aware how little they know of the theory of religion, which we dignify by the name of theology, in contrast to its practice. This means that all too often Dialogue is not really representative of religious Jewry, and so, in spite of its value, may be seriously misleading and therefore dangerous.

Recently in the United States, based especially on Yeshivah

University in New York, there has grown up a positive, militant and philosophical expression of traditional Judaism, which may fairly be called orthodox in the Christian sense. So far, however, it seems to have had little or no effect in Britain, and so, beyond the remark that it is not really representative of Judaism, it may be ignored here. More likely to be met are those who have been influenced by the work of the Lubavitch Chasidim, where sound learning, complete traditionalism and a sprinkling of popular mysticism form an interesting combination. In spite of their zeal, however, they are too demanding in their claims that all life should be a part of religion to gain over many adherents. On the whole they do not seek contacts with Christians. A short mention of Jewish mysticism will be found at the end of the next chapter.

Chapter VIII

THE JEW AT WORSHIP

THE real difference between denominations or different faiths may often be discovered more clearly from their worship than from their credal statements. Yet the evidence has to be handled with discretion, or we may be misled by mere externals. Today Christians are seen in synagogues and Jews in churches far more often than used to be the case, because of the modern stress on dialogue and the type of co-operation promoted by societies like the Council of Christians and Jews. Pulpit interchange is still rare but sufficiently common to call for little comment. There is a tendency, therefore, to comment on non-essentials, e.g. the Jewish man, unless he is very liberal, worships with his head covered; the women, except among the liberals, are segregated; the prayers, etc., except the one for the Queen and the authorities, are in Hebrew or Aramaic, the liberals again making an exception for much of the service—the sermon, of course, is in the language of the country. Such things matter little. Women were segregated in the Temple worship, and in any case this is true also of Christians in a great many countries, even in Europe. Until recently the Church of Rome conducted the liturgy of the Mass in Latin, while in general in the autocephalous Orthodox churches the liturgies tend to be in a language so antiquated as to have the same effect. The Muslim will appreciate the man's covered head as a sign of respect, though, in fact, the chief motive was to be different from Christians.[1]

When one realizes the extent of the congregational participation in all syngogue services, one begins to sense the nature of its worship and, therefore, of Jewish religion better. It should be noted that while old concepts die hard, in the Liberal synagogues the extent of women's participation in-

[1] In the time of Christ the covering or baring of the head during worship was optional among the Jews.

creases steadily, though certain offices are likely to be predominately male for many years to come, and though, at the time of writing, the ordination of the first woman rabbi, Reformed of course, in the United States is announced. In theory women are permitted to hold certain religious offices among the Orthodox and even to be called up to the public reading of the Torah in the synagogue, so the practice is stricter than the theory.

While every synagogue has an established business organization, which, mainly because of its practical nature, has come down little changed from New Testament times, it is under no compulsion to have any religious official. There is no one in it that holds an office even remotely resembling that of a priest or even that of a Protestant minister. There are smaller congregations, especially among the very pious, where even the appearance of a religious leader is avoided.

The rabbi is an expert on the Torah in its widest sense. While he was often chosen because of his spiritual insight, yet he has always been the one who could declare authoritatively what a Jew should or should not do in a given situation. To be noticed, however, is that the rabbi has no authority to enforce his ruling; this is done by the congregation. Normally a rabbi obtains the title by being recognized as such by three acknowledged rabbis. While, under Christian influence, the term ordination is very generally used, it must be understood in the strict sense of appoint; the *shemichah,* the placing (of hands), is only a recognition of what the man knows. It does not confer anything upon him beyond the recognition of his equals. Though it is now rare, a community may choose one of its number to act as its rabbi, because it is convinced of his knowledge,[2] and at least within that community his standing cannot be impugned. It is true that under Christian influence the rabbi is increasingly expected to take on other tasks, especially preaching. It is reasonable to say that the larger and more liberal the synagogue, the more the rabbi is likely to resemble a Christian minister, the smaller and more orthodox the less likely he is. The smaller synagogue in Britain will generally be satisfied with a man of lesser knowledge—*shemichah* is not easy to obtain—who will generally be called the Minister, be addressed in writing as

[2] We might perhaps think of the election of Ambrose as Bishop of Milan by public acclaim.

the Reverend, and may wear a clerical collar, but none of these things approximate him in the least to a Christian minister.

The public services, which can be held only if there are ten Jewish men, not younger than thirteen years old, present may be conducted by anyone of standing. This may, but need not be the rabbi or minister. Where the synagogue can afford it, it is likely to have a permanent official, the Chazzan or Cantor, who may be assisted by a choir (mixed if the synagogue is liberal). His qualification is a knowledge of the traditional melodies and a good (tenor) voice. Even then it is common to give the honour of conducting the introductory portion of the service to one of the synagogue's senior members. The only Christian bodies who are really comparable with the Synagogue in their concept of the equality of the worshippers are smaller groups like the Quakers and Brethren, but they, in contrast to the Jews, eschew all forms of liturgy.

While there are Jews who claim descent from priestly and Levitical families this gives them no special standing in the synagogue. If they are present at a service at which the Torah is read, a *kohen* (priest) will be the first to be called up to read a portion and a Levite will be second, but their absence will not be felt to be a loss by most. The Aaronic blessing can be given only if there are three *kohanim* present. Otherwise their functions are minimal and marginal.

There is nothing in the Synagogue which can really be compared to the Christian sacraments, i.e. a ceremony in which there is an outward and visible sign of an inward and spiritual grace. Circumcision is often compared to infant baptism. Those who practise the latter are convinced that God does something to the baby, either *ex opere operato,* or at least if the conditions proclaimed in the service are carried out, and few of them will claim that the child is in any sense a Christian until it has been baptized. Circumcision is merely the proclaiming that the boy is a Jew and in the covenant; it does not bring him into the covenant, and the ceremony can be postponed, if the doctor thinks it advisable. The *mohel,* who performs the circumcision, will normally be a pious man, but he is chosen for his skill. The prayers at the ceremony are benedictions, i.e. primarily God is praised that man has been enabled to fulfil His command.

Though the Liberal Synagogue calls Bar Mitzvah confirmation and includes girls in its scope the name is seriously misleading. The boy of thirteen, the *bar mitzvah,* i.e. the son of the commandment, simply takes his place as a full Synagogue member, responsible for his own standing before God, by being 'called up' to share in the reading of the Torah. In other words, it is something he does which shows that he is a full member of the family of Israel, purely by virtue of his age.

Marriage is essentially a civil ceremony, though it is accompanied by religious blessings, but it is God that is blessed rather than the bridal pair. Though, again under Christian influence, the ceremony is usually held in the synagogue, a rabbi officiates and a ring is used, none of these things are necessary for a valid marriage. The rites of Passover and Tabernacles are essentially home ones; that which happens in the home is more important than the special Synagogue services.

While the Temple stood, the Synagogue never claimed to be a rival. It existed primarily to foster the study of the Torah and personal piety and outside Jerusalem it also acted as the local community centre, but a man's loyalty was to the Temple, not to the local synagogue. He was expected to say certain standard prayers twice a day, but there was no obligation on him to go to the synagogue for that purpose.[3] The Temple did something for the people; the morning and evening sacrifices were offered irrespective of whether there were any present apart from the officiating priests and Levites. The synagogue existed to enable the individual to perform his religious duties better, and so it could not function unless a quorum (*minyan*) of ten adult males were present, as said above.

When the Temple was destroyed, after the initial shock the rabbis carried on as though nothing had happened. This helps to explain the one-sidedness, from the Christian point of view, of much in the synagogue worship, and this has, in turn, helped to mould the worshipper. Those religious Jews who genuinely feel the absence of sacrifice are few and with few exceptions unrepresentative—for many the suggestion that the sacrificial system should be renewed would be positively

[3] Otherwise Luke need not have said of Jesus that it was His custom to go to the synagogue (4:16).

abhorrent.[4] Equally the concept of the need of a mediator between man and God is confined almost entirely to certain Chasidic groups, where their Tsadik, or rabbi, fills the need—a Chasidic rabbi is a spiritual leader rather than a legal authority. This means that certain stresses, which have always dominated Catholic Christianity, whether in its Roman, Eastern or Protestant forms, have at all times, and today more than ever, seemed strange to normative Jewish religious thinking.

There has been a further result, which is inadequately recognized when Jews and Christians meet in dialogue. The confessions of Paul himself, e.g. in Rom. 7, are sufficient to show that he found no satisfactory solution to the problem of sin in the Judaism that existed before A.D. 70, and that it was only his experience of Christ that enabled him to face it in all its implications and ramifications. For the Christian scholar it is clear enough that while the men of Qumran, the Pharisees and similar groups were extremely concerned with the shortcomings of others in Israel, they were not normally conscious of their own, except in a very limited degree, something which is normally true of Christian groups too. The removal of sacrifice led, almost subconsciously and involuntarily to a further minimizing of sin, and this tendency was increased by the controversy with Christianity and its stress on salvation by the shedding of blood. It should not be forgotten that 'without the shedding of blood there is no forgiveness of sins' (Heb. 9:22) is a good Rabbinic concept, for it is found three times in the Talmud in the form 'No atonement without blood'.[5] Where a weak spot is pressed in controversy, one is apt to retreat from it, and so it has been with the Jew.

Let all this not be misunderstood. One has only to go to the synagogue on Yom Kippur (the Day of Atonement) to realize from the prayers the reality of sin for the religious Jew. But as one listens to the confession of sins great and small, common and rare, one realizes that it is sin as a community

[4] This is something to be remembered, when certain Christian circles speak confidently of the imminent rebuilding of the Temple. Many Jews would hail the erection of a super-synagogue in the Temple area, but a temple is another matter.

[5] *Yoma* 5a, *Menachoth* 93b, *Zebachim* 6a.

matter rather than as an individual problem that is mainly being lamented, something which is probably in conformity with the Old Testament concept of the Day of Atonement. The Synagogue does not really have any adequate answer for the man burdened with a sense of guilt and failure.

The principle involved goes deeper. Though the destruction of the Temple and the resultant vanishing of sacrifices came as a major blow to the Pharisaic party, which soon became dominant in Jewry, and it was confident that it would not be long before it was rebuilt—an attitude that was to last for a century or so—it became increasingly felt that sacrifice was spiritually hardly necessary. Though few traditionalists may be prepared to express it in this way, they indubitably came to feel that sacrifices had ceased because they were no longer necessary. The almost sub-conscious reasoning is that if God has removed the sacrifices, then a great many sins can hardly be so very serious. Many a Jew's attitude is reminiscent of Voltaire's on his death-bed. He is alleged to have said that he was ready to meet his Maker, for "Dieu me pardonera; c'est son métier."[6] It is not that the Jew is sure that his good deeds have outweighed his bad ones, but that he has shown his good will by his keeping of the Torah; God shows His by forgiving the balance, especially on the Day of Atonement.

This scaling down of the seriousness, not of the reality, of sin goes still further. Apart from that of the Incarnation, probably no orthodox Christian doctrine is more repellant to the Jew today, whether he is orthodox or liberal, than that of Original Sin. In New Testament times it would seem that in Alexandrian Jewish circles there was a theory of inherited depravity from Adam, while in Palestine it was rather the tendency to sin from Adam on that was stressed. The classic Rabbinic teaching was that God had implanted two inclinations or impulses in man, one good, one bad (*yetzer ha-tob, yetzer ha-ra*), the latter developed first, but it could be curbed by the study of the Torah. When we compare this with the Christian doctrine, the essential difference is that the evil impulse has been given man as part of his endowment by God; it is not the result of a fall. While the traditionalist Jew is familiar with the classic doctrine, it seems to play little part in his practical teaching. His grateful thanks to God in

[6] Similar words are attributed to Heine in a similar position.

his daily prayer, that He has created his soul pure,[7] is a truer indication of his attitude.

No one can really appreciate Jewish piety unless he has some understanding of the part played by mysticism in it; indeed it is above all this mystical element that has prevented Judaism's becoming the legalistic system so often presented by its detractors. Yet the subject lies outside the scope of this little book.

It is beyond question that Jews played a part in that great syncretistic, Hellenistic movement called normally by the all-embracing name of Gnosticism, and it has been argued by Jewish scholars that behind those forms of it that specially influenced Christianity Jewish circles may be traced. Be that as it may, though the rabbis took good care not to preserve their literature, it is clear that during the second century A.D. even leading figures in Jewish orthodoxy experimented with it, and through them a certain mystic tradition entered the synagogue.

Ever since then it has been a live factor in Judaism, especially in times of the bitterest persecution, e.g. under the Spanish Inquisition. It has always been regarded with suspicion by some rabbis, and those under thirty have been discouraged from or even forbidden its study. Sometimes it has been of an essentially Gnostic type, sometimes anti-intellectual. It has very often seemed to be on the verge of pantheism, but the Biblical stress on God's transcendence has always held it back, just as the Synagogue's stress on the Torah has kept it from antinomianism. In the later eighteenth century this mysticism found a possibly unique expression in a movement known as Chasidism. For once mysticism was offered as a popular mass movement. Though it later degenerated in large part into superstition, it gave new life to the East-European Synagogue at a time when its spiritual life seemed to be at its most arid. Even today the Lubaivitch Chasidim, mentioned earlier, represents a major possibility of spiritual renewal within Jewry. Though his interpretation of Chasidism has been challenged, probably correctly, because he omitted elements repugnant to modern thought, it was one of the foundation stones in the spiritual life of Martin Buber.

[7] O my God, the soul which Thou gavest me is pure; Thou didst create it, Thou didst form it, Thou didst breathe it into me.

Because of the complexity of the subject no description can be attempted here.[8] What is, however, important is that one should never assume that the theological points stressed in earlier chapters are the sole constituents of every Jew's religion. The mystic element, where found, can have a strongly transforming power on the traditional building blocks. Indeed, for a small, but significant group the Kabbalah, proved the bridge which led to Christ.

[8] Those interested are referred to Gershom Scholem, *Major Trends in Jewish Mysticism*, and to its Bibliography.

Chapter IX

THE NATIONAL JEW

IN the world in which the prophets proclaimed "Thus saith the LORD" it was an obvious truism that a man had virtually no opportunity of learning of the God of Israel unless he lived in the land of Israel, and had even less chance of carrying out His will unless he lived among the people of Israel, the more so as the Torah is the expression of the covenant with Israel rather than a universal moral revelation. The story of Ruth in the time of Judges and of Achior in the book of Judith, written in the second century B.C. (see especially 14:10), show that at no time was any obstacle placed in the way of a Gentile's being taken into the covenant people, if there was a genuine acceptance of its God. It was its religion rather than its blood that created Israel.

There were, however, major social difficulties in the way of a man, in contrast to a woman, who wanted to be accepted in Israel, for, unless he had entered the royal service, it was almost impossible for him to acquire land, without which he could not rank as a full citizen. So, after the initial admixture of Canaanite and Amorite blood that followed on the Conquest, the number of additions to the population from outside was probably small, and the fiction of relative racial purity could grow up. While Ezra's drastic action in dissolving mixed marriages should almost certainly be interpreted in the light of Mal. 2:10-16, Neh. 13:23-27, i.e. the foreign wives in question had not accepted the worship of Israel's God, yet the dangerous term 'the holy seed' (Ezr. 9:2, RSV 'holy race') is found. That this undercurrent existed is shown by John the Baptist's warning "Do not begin to say to yourselves 'We have Abraham as our father' " (Lk. 3:8).

The paramount stress on religion rather than physical descent is shown in the fact that John Hyrcanus (134-104 B.C.) gave the Edomites who had settled in Idumea, i.e. southern Judea, the choice of accepting Judaism or exile, and the same policy was followed by his son Aristobulus I (104-103 B.C.) when he added Galilee to the Hasmonean kingdom. If the usual estimate of the Jewish population of the Roman empire in the time of Augustus is correct, it is clear that a great many proselytes must have been won, especially in the Near-East. Josephus tells us how the royal house of Adiabene, in Northern Mesopotamia, accepted Judaism. This trend, which even while the Temple stood made the Diaspora the normal form of life for a majority of Jews, was reversed by the conditions under which Jews lived after the time of Constantine and the rise of Islam. The conversion of a Christian or a Muslim, according to the circumstances, normally meant death for the converter and converted alike, so Judaism perforce ceased to be a missionary religion. In addition, most Jews down to the Emancipation—many down to 1914, and in some Muslim lands virtually down to the present day—either had to or found it advisable to live a segregated life, sometimes even in a specially walled section of the city (the ghetto). This meant that it was virtually impossible for a man to be a Jew religiously without being one nationally, or to be one nationally without at least claiming to be one religiously.

The coming of emancipation had a major disruptive force on traditional Jewry. Many claimed to be French, Germans, English, Americans, etc. of the Mosaic faith, while others cast off their links with Jewry and accepted Christianity either out of conviction or to facilitate assimilation. Yet others embraced the new faith of Marxism; whether they maintained their claim to Jewish nationality or proclaimed themselves citizens of the world depended on circumstances. It is difficult to forecast what the effects of this movement, visible wherever Jews received full citizen rights, would have been on Jewry, had it not been nipped in the bud by the wave of political antisemitism which began in Germany in 1873 and spread rapidly to Austria and France, both traditional centres of dislike of the Jews on religious grounds. It was eagerly embraced by Russia, also a traditional home of dislike of the Jews. It produced the pogroms, which began in 1881 and continued down to the 1914 war. The policy of the czars to kill one third of Russia's Jews, force one third out of the country and the remainder to baptism led to the sudden growth of America's Jewry on the one hand[1] and on the other

[1] A very high proportion of Britain's Jewry is also derived from this source.

to the turning of the rather idealistic Zionist movement into a viable organization. In the West antisemitism gradually convinced most Jews that assimilation was impossible. With the outbreak of the Nazi holocaust, which probably claimed six million direct victims—those indirectly affected cannot be calculated—it became emotionally almost impossible to disassociate oneself nationally from one's fellow Jews, however little one felt oneself actively involved. After the Six-Day War of 1967 world Jewry felt stirred with pride at such an overwhelming victory even in circles where intellect dictated a rejection of a Jewish state. So today nationalism, in some form or another, is probably a stronger and further-reaching influence in Jewry than religion.

The Zionist movement normally looks to Theodor Herzl as its founder, though he had predecessors, and the first of the modern Jewish settlements in Palestine dates back to 1882. He was born in 1860 in Budapest. He grew up a free-thinker and a sharer in the optimisitic romanticism of the late nineteenth century. His Jewish origin had little meaning for him and his ancestors' religion even less. He studied in Vienna and became a journalist there, meeting repeatedly with antisemitism in the widest strata of the population. He was able to discount it by saying that the liberal principles of the French Revolution had yet to be absorbed into the despotic system of the Hapsburg Austro-Hungarian empire. When he had to cover the Dreyfus case in France, he realized with a shock that the evil spirits of the past were as active in Republican France as in Imperial Austria or Russia.

The solution to this problem he put forward in *Der Judenstaat*. (The Jewish State) in 1896 and at the first Zionist Congress in Basel the following year. He maintained that antisemitism was caused primarily by the particularity of the Jew and that this should be removed by his acquiring a homeland like all other peoples. He might, if he wished, continue to live outside this land, holding to his religion, if he so desired, but he would have an acknowledged nationality and a refuge where he could go in time of need. All this was before the time of visas and even of passports in the more civilized countries.

There was an immediate adverse reception from most quarters. The stress on nationality at a time when the liberal was increasingly stressing the international and supra-national saddened not a few Jews. Others saw their newly-won status as full citizens threatened. The liberal in religion saw his dream of Judaism as the all-pervasive true religion undermined. On the whole, however, the reaction from the Westernized liberal wing tended to apathy rather than active opposition. This came from the orthodox side, for the rabbis saw that Zionism was essentially a betrayal of Judaism. It was a repetition of the call of Israel to Samuel to make the people like all the nations. In addition it made religion something optional; it was no longer to be the one and only motivation for Jewry's existence. Some of the rabbis launched excommunications against those that might support Herzl.

It was the unexpected mass support from Russia and neighbouring lands that saved the infant movement. The more than six million Jews of Russia had been under mounting persecution and the pressure of growing poverty ever since 1786. For the first time since the expulsion of the Jews from Spain in the fifteenth century the Synagogue failed to hold the loyalty of many of its adherents. Martyrdom they could have faced with equanimity, but the continuing pressure of anti-Jewish measures wore away the fibre of religious resistance. Many turned to nationalism, socialism or the revolutionary movement, with greater or less, explicit or implicit rejection of traditional religion.

It was from these circles that an enthusiastic welcome came for the Zionist dream, but in welcoming it they also transformed it. The pre-1914 settlers in Palestine for the most part combined a fervent socialist vision of a new earth in which righteousness dwells with their nationalism. The famous Zionist discovery of the kibbutz, the communal colony, was an adaptation of this vision to the practical exigencies of pioneering life. There were always in addition also synagogue members prepared to face the objections of the ultra-pious and to join the movement as observant Jews. As early as 1901 the Mizrachi movement was founded to represent them and their interests, and it has been the religious wing of Zionism ever since. On the whole, however, religion has played little part in Zionism.

These early settlers provided the leaders who headed the Yishub, the organized Jewish community in Palestine, when Britain received the Mandate. In the later inter-war years they increasingly took over the leadership of the Zionist movement as a whole. Since the setting up of the State of Israel the foundations they laid have proved adequate for the greater edifice built on them.

The development of the Yishub after 1919 was deeply influenced by two unforeseen events. It lost the impetus of the millions in Russia, who found themselves barred from emigration and it had to face massive opposition from the Palestinian Arabs.[2] The latter caused Britain to restrict immigration either by demanding that the immigrant had considerable capital available or by fixing annual quotas for non-capitalists. The latter were handled by the Zionist organization so those they brought in were those considered to be most suitable as pioneering settlers, but this meant disappointing many older and more zealous supporters of the movement.

Zionism might have lost its grip on the Jewish masses, had Hitler not come to power in 1933. Though perhaps a third of the one and a half million Jews of Germany and Austria were able to find refuge in various countries, it soon became clear that for most of them the only places of refuge were Palestine, Shanghai,[3] or the grave. When war and "the final solution" came, Shanghai was no longer available. It was Palestine or the gas chambers, and few there were that reached the former either directly or through British prison camps.

There is no Jew we are likely to meet, whether religious or irreligious, whether a nationalist or a citizen of the world, who has not had these experiences burnt indelibly into his consciousness. Even the strongest opponents of Zionism loosened their purse-strings to help the survivors to get to Palestine and then to support the State of Israel. The victories of 1947-48, of 1957 and above all of 1967 created virtually everywhere a deep national pride in being a Jew, even where there was not the slightest intention of letting it conflict with their British, American, or other nationality.

[2] No effort should be made to deny that Britain entered into mutually incompatible obligations to King Hussain of the Hedjaz and to the Jews through the Balfour Declaration. We may doubt whether any members of the British Cabinet were really aware of this; certainly the Jewish leaders were not. Both strangely thought that Palestine was almost unpopulated.

[3] There were no immigration laws controlling the International Settlement in Shanghai. Of course, most who reached it could find no work.

The brief honeymoon of many Jews with Russian communism was brought to a permanent end with the virulent antisemitism of Stalin's later years. It is remarkable that the leaders of the agitation in Russia to be allowed to leave for Israel are those with little or no contact with the Synagogue; most of them are known for their contribution to the welfare of Russia in war and peace. Even the most fanatically orthodox Jews, though they still have their heart-searchings about the state and condemn the government's non-religious policy, have with few exceptions forgotten their old ban on the Zionist movement.

All this means that an emotional, often irrational, link exists between ninety per cent of Jews and the State of Israel. Whereas a century ago it was still religion that was the outstanding mark of most Jews, above all it is nationalism today. Hence in the meeting of Jew and Christian, the interest has largely shifted from the question whether the Christian Gospel is compatible with the Jewish heritage to the only half-expressed problem of whether it is possible for a Jew to be a Christian and yet remain a Jew. In the famous Father Daniel case (1962) the Israel Supreme Court decided that a Jew who had accepted Christianity could no longer be regarded as a Jew for the purposes of statute law, even though he remained one by rabbinic definition. In fact, however, the decision was badly received by many. The reason for the changing attitude is the Hebrew-Christian movement, which has been gathering strength for the past century, and whose main expression is the International Hebrew Christian Alliance. Its main purpose is not theological, for its basis is orthodox Christianity; its main insistence is that a Jew who comes to faith in Christ has the right to remain a Jew nationally and has a continuing responsibility to his people.

The influence of nationalism in contrast to religion is likely to increase rather than decrease among the Jews. This is partly because traditional Judaism has found itself signally incapable of adapting itself to the new situation created by the State of Israel. It is clear that many of the younger generation would be prepared to find room for some form of religion in their general approach to life, the more so as Russian hostility to Israel over the years has seriously tarnished the image of communism generally. But the leadership of the Synagogue in Israel is in the hands of all or nothing men—

we may ask whether traditional Judaism is really capable of compromise where the Torah is concerned. Reform Judaism has no official status whatever. In addition, however, its particular outlook seems as irrelevant to most of the younger generation as is that of orthodoxy. So Israel is religiously Jewish only in the sense that Britain is Christian. Circumcision is a national sign that is carried out automatically in the maternity hospital. Jewish bakers are not allowed to bake leavened bread during Passover, and Jewish butchers sell officially only such meat as has been approved and slaughtered according to rabbinic regulations. Businesses and factories close on the Sabbath, except where the national interest declares otherwise. The great festivals are public holidays. The Old Testament, and fairly often parts of the New, are taught as history and part of the national heritage. Many are orthodox in the sense that they keep the Torah, when it is reasonable to do so, as a professor of the University of Jerusalem said to me. The country is neither pagan nor openly atheist, but its religion, apart from a relatively small minority, is a colouring rather than a reality. What is true of Israel is true of most Jewish communities.

Chapter X

THE CHRISTIAN UNDER THE SHADOW OF THE PAST

SOME wit has said that whenever I hold a conversation with another person there are in fact six involved. There is I as I think myself to be, I as the other thinks me to be, and I as I really am; the same applies, of course, to the other person involved. This principle is least applicable, when the man with whom I talk is either very well known to me or completely unknown, because then there are fewest chances of preconceptions. The main difficulty in Jewish-Christian dialogue is that these two peoples have walked side by side for so much of the way. They have eyed one another from opposite sides of the road, but they have very seldom become intimate. The knowledge of one another they think they have has normally been distorted and distorting.

After a Jewish state in Palestine had completely and finally vanished with the crushing of Bar Kochba's revolt (A.D. 132-135) and the Jewish-Christian Church, the fragments of which were regarded as heretical, had withered away into insignificance, the main contacts between Christians and Jews were in the midst of Hellenistic Greek culture. Already then the primacy of reason in Christian faith was being stressed; a man's profession of faith was regarded mainly as an intellectual act, not as the work of the Holy Spirit working in ways unknowable to men. Hence the heretic was regarded either as mentally deficient or as a bad man, generally the latter. This helps to explain why he was accused with monotonous regularity of unnameable moral crimes. It is easy to undersand that the same attitude was taken up against the Jew, who refused to listen to the preaching of the Gospel and had crucified the Lord of glory. Already in Chrysostom (347-417) we find most of the accusations which are to recur with monotonous regularity down to our own day.[1]

[1] A selection of his accusations will be found in the Additional Note to this chapter.

Just as there have been Jews who were good men, so there have been those who were bad, though the proportion of good to bad has probably been better than in the average Christian church—after all, the discipline of the Law has had its effect. As Hillaire Belloc pointed out in his much misunderstood book on the Jew, the very fact that Jewish badness is apt to be other than the forms taken by surrounding Gentile badness makes the Jewish form more obvious, but not necessarily worse. Exactly the same can be seen in many of the accusations made against coloured immigrants into Britain.

There is no evidence that Chrysostom was basing his attacks on any personal contacts with or experience of Jews. He was simply following the high *a priori* road that Eliphaz the Temanite took with Job (ch. 22). Job was suffering beyond measure, therefore he was a sinner beyond measure, and therefore he must have committed all the sins Eliphaz thought most heinous. In the same way the Jews had lost land and Temple, and this could only be because they had rejected and crucified Jesus and were continuing to reject Him, and this in turn meant that they must be utterly depraved. So the Patriarch of Antioch drew a picture of depraved people as he thought they must be.

The only reason for my laying any stress on Chrysostom is that he was the first of whom we know to draw a picture of the Jew as he ought to be, not as he was. The details were to vary down the centuries, depending on circumstances and the imagination and grossness of the verbal painter, until they reached probably their limit in Streicher's obscenities in *Der Stürmer* under Hitler, but the principle remained the same.

This has been the attitude of the Christian Church towards the Jews virtually throughout its history and has affected every denomination, though not always to the same extent and with the same brutality. In many cases it has confined itself mainly to a denigration of the religion of the Synagogue, in which neither life nor value could be seen. This is not a dislike and suspicion of the Jew because he is one nationally, but because he is not a Christian; it may even be combined with an unwise lionizing of the Hebrew-Christian. Let it be stressed that this is not antisemitism, though it may prepare the soil for it. It is a theological attitude based on theological presuppositions; for clarity it may be called anti-Judaism, though this term too is open to misunderstanding. While anti-semitism has grown in ground prepared by anti-Judaism, its roots derive from national and racial prejudices in which religion plays little or no part. It is as real in communist Russia as it ever was in nominally Christian Germany.

Officially anti-Judaism no longer exists today. Christians are supposed to have been so shocked by the results of antisemitism under the Nazis, that it is assumed that they have abandoned every prejudice against the Jew. Yet survey after survey have shown that the old stereotypes live on, especially where the Jew is least known. Where they have genuinely disappeared, it has normally been on humanistic grounds, only in many cases to be replaced by a foolish and undiscriminating praise of the Jew, which in the end leads only to worse misunderstanding. The stronger the Biblical interest in a church or denomination the stronger the probability of anti-Jewish prejudice (and of support for Jewish missions!) and the greater the probability of its indoctrination at Sunday School level.[2]

Anti-Judaism has been from the first, as has already been said, a theological phenomenon, a response to a theological problem, however much it has borne bitter fruit in the social sphere. Real relations between a Christian and a Jew on anything deeper than a humanistic level—no belittling of the humanistic level is intended—demand from the Christian a thorough understanding of the theological issues involved, unless, indeed, both parties are so liberal as to deny uniqueness in their religion. There are certain traditional theologies which are by the very nature of their formulation anti-Judaistic, for they implicitly deny the possibility of God's gracious presence in the Synagogue. They can be corrected only by a return to the teaching of the New Testament, which finds its classic expression in Rom. 9-11. In older commentaries the tendency is either virtually to ignore these chapters, or to force on them a meaning Paul cannot possibly have intended. It is remarkable to what extent the treatment of these chapters has changed, the turning point being perhaps the commentary by Sanday and Headlam.[3] A true understanding of them will eliminate any feeling of superiority from

[2] For a careful study of the subject see the survey of the American scene in B. E. Olson, *Faith and Prejudice* (Yale University Press).

[3] My little book, *The Mystery of Israel*, is a serious attempt to grapple with the problems involved.

the Christian and prevent any *a priori* spiritual condemnation of the Jew.

It caused a major furore in the United States, when in 1969 Black Power demanded a reparation payment of $500 million —a figure afterwards considerably increased—from the Christian churches. Whatever the reaction of the denominational leaders, that of the ordinary church member was one of more or less amused indignation. This was not due to a denial that the black man had been unreasonably and wrongly treated, but that the claims to reparation were being posted to the wrong address.

The Jewish community, whether represented by the World Zionist Organization or by the World Jewish Congress, or by any other body, ministerial or lay, has no thought of handling in a bill for reparations to anyone, however justified it might be, though the feeling is often met that the churches should do more to help the charitable aspect of Zionism. It is all too easily forgotten how heavy the burden shouldered by the young state of Israel was, when it accepted the physically and mentally broken survivors of the concentration camps without any qualifications. When one hears that over a million immigrants have entered Israel since the State was set up, one is apt to forget how high a proportion of them had to be aided by the state rather than aiding it.

What those Jews who are really in touch with the churches, perhaps relatively few in number, but influential beyond their numerical proportion, would like to hear is a frank confession by the churches, not merely that the Jews have been wronged by the Christian world, but also and even more by the churches. This has been done in a half-hearted way by the Second Vatican Council, though those Jews who know the Roman Church well realize that little more could have been expected from a church claiming infallibility. It is tragic, however, that those political currents which were side-tracked by able organization at Vatican II have been successful in preventing the World Council of Churches from making any adequate statement on the subject. It has, of course, repeatedly condemned antisemitism, as it has all forms of racism, and has demanded that it should be combatted, but this has not been a recognition that behind anti-semitism lies something that is peculiarly the Church's creation, viz. anti-Judaism.

The effects of this may be far more subtle and far-reaching

than is often realized. In Germany, and in some other European countries also, there are many devoted Christians who consider that they are debarred from presenting Christ to the Jews because of the complicity of their churches in antisemitism, positively or by silent acquiescence. They may give much money and loving service to various forms of reparation, which, however, virtually exclude the possibility of verbal witness. To place the Jew outside the terms of the Great Commission is ultimately to deny him his place as man among men.

There are others who are so committed to Dialogue, which involves those who take part in it meeting as equals in every sense, that they abandon every claim to uniqueness and finality in Christianity. This does not take them very far, for it becomes a virtual invitation to the Jew involved to deny any uniqueness or finality in his faith as well. Dialogue can become fully meaningful only when one sits down with others, regarding them with respect and as one's equals, but yet believing that one has something unique to share with them—not to force upon them. The remarkable feature of our time is the number of Jews who have recognized that Jesus may be able to give to the Gentile something that Judaism cannot offer him. There are even those who will acknowledge in confidence, that owing to errors in upbringing or to weaknesses in the life of the local Jewish community there are *some* Jews who need Jesus, so that He may meet needs the Synagogue cannot satisfy. True dialogue must not assume that all faiths are variants of the one truth, but that the other has so experienced truth, that it has profoundly transformed him, and so I may have something to learn from him that may enrich me. Where dialogue has been carried on in this spirit, though no change in religious allegiance may have taken place, both sides have profited and have probably come to a deeper understanding of their own faith.

Throughout the world during the past three decades there has been a growing attack on Christian missionary work. To a great extent this has been nationalistically or ideologically motivated,[4] but all too often there have been deeper and more justifiable reasons. Very often it has been an objection to the

[4] The State of Israel has from the first adopted a far more reasonable and liberal attitude towards Christian missionaries and missions than the vast majority of Asian and African countries.

messenger and his methods rather than to his message, and fairness compels us to acknowledge that it has often been justified. Men and women have been employed on the mission field who would not have been welcomed by the church at home, and consciously or unconsciously advantage has been taken of the hearer's physical or economic distress, while the message may well be linked with the fast-waning prestige of Western civilization. At the same time the extent of this has been greatly exaggerated. Sometimes it has been due to the zeal of inexperience and the lack of adequate training, sometimes to the passionate desire to meet desperate human need, where the emotions have been allowed to take control, but one bad apple may taint a whole case.

The more a Jew knows true Christianity, the more he expects the Christian to be a missionary, for he knows that missionary work belongs to the very nature of the Church. He will speak, too, in the highest terms of some missionaries he has known. For all that he will consistently attack the very existence of Jewish missions. For this there are many reasons, of which only some of the more important can be mentioned.

Such a Jew knows full well that apart from a few denominations, e.g., the Moravians and the Christian and Missionary Alliance, missionary work has been a marginal activity within the Church, and that Jewish missionary work has normally been the Cinderella. Hostility to Jewish missions is normally stronger among British Jews than in most other countries just because they know that the average minister has no real interest in him and the average church member even less. I have no wish to criticise missionary methods, because the informed critic knows that the chief offenders have to be looked for outside Britain, and that the charge of buying converts has had less applicability here than most lands. In using the term "buying converts" I am not justifying the accusation. The "rice Christian" has very seldom been motivated purely by financial considerations. He is the victim of intolerable economic conditions, who has responded to what may well have been the first altruistic interest and love he has met, but the very fact that his community has been unable or unwilling to help him makes it resent his departure the more.[5]

[5] Jewish philanthropy is so admirable, that many do not realise how many Jewish communities broke down under the burden of mass poverty and need from 1880 onwards.

The Christian may have to apologize for his church and for its methods, but he need not apologize for his message or for bringing it not in dialogue but as a missionary, for otherwise the majority of Jews will not hear it. What he should listen to is the Jewish accusation, so seldom spoken aloud, but normally the heart of the attack, "You are not really concerned with my believing in Jesus; you want me to cease being a Jew." In spite of the advance of secularization, very many Jews in the West still accept the equation Gentile=Christian. Since their own Jewish observance may well be minimal, they regard the Christmas tree and the hot-cross-bun as symbols of genuine Christianity. So he does not realize that becoming a Christian means being a member of a minority; he thinks it involves becoming a Gentile, a national renegade.

Is he so far wrong? Is not this what so many Christians think and want? Today the indigenization of the Church is everywhere the parrot cry, as though nationality were the sole determining factor in the welfare of the local church. But let someone urge the need of a Hebrew-Christian church, and all the ecclesiastical dove-cotes are a-flutter.[6] The racial memory of more than a millennium clamours that one may be a British, American, German, Japanese, Bantu, Indian, etc., Christian, but a Hebrew Christian, no!

This is perhaps the supreme challenge the Jew brings to us, as we stand under the shadow of the past. Either let us be really supra-national, neither Greek nor Jew, neither bond nor free, neither male nor female, or let us regard the Jew as we regard any other man and accept that his faith in Christ does not touch his nationality, and that he may express his nationality in the working out of his faith like any other man. I personally prefer the former path, but since there are few that walk it in practice, I accept that the Hebrew Christian has his fully equal national place in the Church of Christ. When I seek to bring the Jew the message of Jesus, his Messiah, I must seek by every means in my power not to gentilize him, not to detach him from his people and his national loyalties. I cannot forbid his assimilation, but I have

[6] Outside Israel there are in fact very few advocates of such a church. In Israel, while it will never be a solely Jewish church, yet it is bound to become, sooner or later, essentially a Hebrew Christian church, with Hebrew as the predominant language of worship. Further prophecy is premature.

no right to aid and encourage it. It could even be that the Hebrew Christian points the way to the solution of much of the racialism that injures and poisons the Church so deeply today.

ADDITIONAL NOTE

CHRYSOSTOM ON THE JEWS

ST. JOHN CHRYSOSTOM, then Patriarch of Antioch, preached eight sermons against the Jews in 386 and 387. Only an indication of the charges he brings against them can be given.

The Jews had rejected the blessings God had heaped on them. They had been adopted sons but are now like dogs. They anger God both by the breach and the keeping of the Law. Stiff-necked, they had broken the easy yoke of Christ, and so are like beasts without reason. They are drunkards and gluttonous. Like a worthless bullock, incapable of work, they are fit only for the butchers.

Of the Synagogue he said, "If you call it a brothel, a den of vice, the Devil's refuge, Satan's fortress, a place to deprave the soul, an abyss of every conceivable disaster or whatever else you will, you are still saying less than it deserves." He claimed that the Old Testament Scriptures had been brought into the synagogues, "not to honour them, but to insult them, and to dishonour them".

On the basis of Ps. 106:37 he claimed that "they sacrificed their sons and daughters to devils; they outraged nature, and overthrew from their foundations the laws of relationship. They are become worse than the wild beasts, and for no reason at all with their own hands they murder their own offspring, to worship the avenging devils who are the foes of our life." He claimed that the Jews worship not God but devils.

We hear the charge of deicide, and we are told that God hates them and indeed has always hated them. Therefore it is the duty of Christians to hate them too. Need we be surprised, if the Church carried out such teaching to the letter, and there is a short step from such denunciations of the synagogues to their destruction?

Chapter XI

THE JEW UNDER THE SHADOW OF THE PAST

IT is obvious that if the Christian approaches the Jew under the burden of centuries of misunderstanding and misjudgment, the same is bound to be true of the Jew. This book, however, is not addressed to Jews, and therefore it does not ask whether they need to get Christians into better focus. In fact they do; their ignorance of Christians and Christianity is often lamentable, but it is for a Jew to tell them where they must change their ideas.

Here the previous chapter is being repeated but in darker colours. Its facts are recalled, not as a truly regretful Christian might state them, but as a Jew has felt them, often all too personally. For that reason a certain amount of repetition is unavoidable. On the other hand this is not a history of the persecution of the Jews. What is mentioned is intended only to give certain salient points, to refer to certain depths of infamy and suffering. For the rest reference must be made to the Bibliography. We must begin, however, by trying briefly to see what the Jew thinks about himself.

The psychologist and sociologist are much concerned today with the problem of racial memory and its effects. One remarkable feature of Jewry is that normally its world-wide dispersion has done little to lessen or diversify this memory. Culturally Jews vary tremendously, but so far as one can judge, their world-outlook tends to be remarkably similar. This has been due partly to the 'ghetto' system, which turned Jews in on themselves for so long, and partly to the dislike, and worse, with which they have been regarded by Christian and Muslim alike.

The Synagogue has no real theory of election—statements on the subject in the Talmud and Midrashim are not self-consistent—and the average Jew has no real concept of the goal of his election beyond the fact that it is bound up with the coming of the Kingdom of God on earth. Above all, for him the stress is not on him as an individual but as a member of the elect people of God. When election is taken seriously by a Christian, there is always the danger of its being expressed in personal and heavenly terms only. It is a notorious fact, that even the return of Christ may, where it is taken seriously, be regarded over much in terms of the individual. The refrain of a popular Second Advent hymn, "That will be glory, glory for me", shows this by subtly shifting the stress from the Saviour to the saved.

Though the Synagogue has not escaped its periods of counting dates and interpreting the signs of the times, these, on the whole, have played little part in its thinking. Rather it has seen the Jew in the centre of the movement of world history towards its predestined end. Hence the average religious Jew is less concerned with individual salvation than is his Christian neighbour, and his belonging to his people will probably mean more to him than a Christian's belonging to his church. This fact will almost certainly deeply colour any Jew's approach to dialogue with a Christian.

When Jew and Christian meet, the latter is apt to be influenced by what he *thinks* the Jew is and what he *thinks* he has done; that is why it is so hard to pin down the anti-Jewish Christian to a specific charge against a Jew or group of Jews. The Jew is influenced by what Christians have done. He can almost always refer to specific things done to himself, and he has a long and well-authenticated list of horrors and injustices to back up his charge. Let us hear the almost casual testimony of a Jewess, brought up with the minimum of religion and Jewish knowledge, when in the midst of atheism and with a communist past she had to face the claims of Christ as presented by her husband:

> I knew all the history of Christian persecution of my people. How Jews were forcibly baptized, and how they had killed their own children, and then themselves, in thousands, rather than change their religion. How they were forced to listen to Catholic Masses, and stopped their ears to avoid hearing what they considered blasphemy . . . Few outsiders can guess how strong a hold anti-Christian feelings may have on a Jewish heart. Besides the historical reasons, there were nearly always personal ones. As a child I had to walk home from school past a corner where two bigger girls lay in wait

to pull my hair 'because you're a dirty little Jewess'.[1] This testimony may have the more effect because of its essentially incidental nature.

The one festival that is observed in a real sense by the majority of Jews is Passover. In a recent poll 87% of those interrogated claimed to observe Yom Kippur (the Day of Atonement), 86% Rosh Hashanah (New Year's Day), 79% Passover. The observance of Rosh Hashanah need be no more than social and that of Yom Kippur is all too often purely negative; that of Passover, however, must by its very nature be positive. In addition, modern nationalistic trends have encouraged its being kept in wider group settings and not merely as a home ceremony.

For the Christian Passover is the festival of liberation from Egyptian bondage. For the Jew, however, there are many overtones and undertones. A Passover *hagadah* (the name given to the service book) in my possession—a simple one that has probably circulated in tens of thousands of copies—shows in its illustrations not merely the Egyptian taskmaster, but also a soldier who could be equally well an Assyrian or Babylonian, a Roman legionary, a mail-clad Crusader knight balanced by a friar with a crucifix and sword and between them an ordinary man killing a Jew, a Cossack with a knout, who speaks alike of Chmielnicki in the 17th century, who wiped out 744 Jewish communities, of Haimaduks in the 18th century, of the Russian pogrom and of the Petlura massacres in 1919. Finally we are shown a storm-trooper dragging a Jew to a concentration camp. The *hagadah* could have added, had it so chosen, that Passover was the season when the dreaded blood libel was apt to be heard, that the Jews had killed a Christian child to mix its blood into the flour and water of the mazzot (unleavened bread) of the festival.

The Jews no longer wince at the memory of Nebuchadnezzar and Titus, for all that they stood for has long since crumbled to dust. The arch of Titus, near the Forum in Rome, stands more as a tribute to the Jew than to the man who erected it. But the Crusaders and the armed mob, the Inquisition and the pogrom—what they represented is still with us, even though half-hidden. The Vatican has never denounced the Inquisition as having been rotten in root and branch, and

[1] Sabina Wurmbrand, ***The Pastor's Wife.***

even after the Czarist regime fell, its supporters carried its forgery, *The Protocols of the Elders of Zion,* with them until an even darker power took it over.

Few Jews blame the storm-trooper on the Christian, and the more they know of Hitler's methods, the less they blame the Church in Germany for not realizing his aims at the very beginning. After the Nuremberg Laws of 1935, however, they should have been clear. After the night of 9-10 November 1938, when almost all the synagogues were burnt, and the Jewish community was ruined by a tremendous communal fine, ignorance could only be deliberate. Yet how small the reaction was. Not a few Germans figure on the roll of Righteous Gentiles in Jerusalem among those who risked and often lost their lives to help the Jews, but the normal reaction was helpless submission. In spite of Hochhuth's justified attack on the Vatican in *The Deputy,* it is probable that the Roman Catholics did more than the Lutheran Church of Germany, though this did produce the Confessional Church—a better rendering is the Confessing Church—and this in turn did more than the numerically weak Free Churches.

Probably many such Jews blame the churches outside Germany more than they do those inside. The churches in Holland and above all Denmark showed in the hour of crisis what could be done, when Christians set their hearts on it and risked their lives. But where Hitler's writ did not run, it is tragic how little was achieved. We must never forget that more than three quarters of a million and a half Jews in Germany and Austria might have been saved instead of only about a third, had there been more financial giving and more pressure on governments, professional associations and trade unions. One of the most respected Jewish scientists in England, Dr. C. Singer, was strongly attracted to Jesus, but at the last he sadly and reluctantly turned his back on the Church, not because it had done so little for German Jews, but because it had neglected the German Hebrew Christian in his need.

In the early Middle Ages England was neither better nor worse than other European countries in its treatment of its Jewish community, though because of the country's commercial backwardness the number of Jews was relatively small. It solved its Jewish 'problem' in the typical way by expelling its Jews in 1290, after having stripped them of almost all their possessions. It did not readmit them until 1655. Even then the move was so potentially unpopular that the permission was not made public till 1664. Though the small Jewish community was little interfered with, the Jewish Naturalization Bill of 1753 aroused such opposition that it was repealed the same year. Their disabilities—in some ways less onerous than those of the Dissenters—began to be removed in 1829; Moses Montefiore became a knight in 1837, but British Jewry had to wait until 1858 for Lionel de Rothschild to be allowed to take his seat in parliament, and until 1885 for his son, Nathaniel Rothschild, to become the first Jewish peer. On the other hand, we should remember that though only a relatively small number of fleeing Russian Jews reached Britain, the Aliens Act of 1905 had the keeping down of their number as one of its chief purposes.

It follows that the normal British Jew need have few bitter thoughts about Britain itself, something that is borne out by the relatively small emigration to Israel. But the majority of its Jews are descended from those that entered the country after 1880, and they look back to parents and grandparents and many other relations who suffered and perished in Russia, Rumania, Poland, Hungary and Germany and they cannot help thinking of what we might have done, had our gates been wider open.

When 1961 came round, there were many who hoped that the Church of England might officially and publically express its regrets for the expulsion of so many Dissenting ministers three hundred years earlier on St. Bartholomew's Day. It is true that some men in high position took advantage of the occasion to express their regrets for the mistake and indeed the wrong done then by the Church of England, but their action made the silence of official circles the more obvious. In just the same way the Jew would like the churches today not merely to repudiate antisemitism, as indeed most have done, but also to acknowledge their failures and shortcomings in the past. The Lutheran churches in Germany have made an unreserved confession of their blame for much that happened to the Jews in the Nazi period and of their failure to stand up for right. But there has been no *unreserved* retraction of so much anti-Judaistic expression in the past, including the notorious anti-Jewish outbursts by Martin Luther; indeed, repeatedly efforts are made to excuse and even justify him.

It is typical that during the Second Vatican Council a number of publications were issued seeking to affect its decisions, in which many of the old calumnies against the Jews were once again repeated.

One more example, on a much more excusable level, must suffice. A strong and reasonably representative and international, theological working party drew up a report for the Bristol meeting (1967) of the Faith and Order department of the W.C.C. on "The Church and the Jewish People".[2] The great weakness of the group was that it included few who were in close contact with the Jewish outlook. So in spite of the fact that it was a careful and serious piece of work by men and women who were conscious of the Church's guilt where the Jew is concerned, and who therefore chose their language with care, the unanimous opinion of Jews was that its conclusions were hopelessly vitiated by the way in which they were expressed. True enough, it was not composed for Jewish readers, but as part of the published report of the Bristol meeting, it was available to any who wished to buy it. In fact, some of the worst crudities were removed by the work of an independent sub-committee more aware of the tensions, but no more than minor verbal alterations were possible. Thus one more well-meaning attempt lost much of its value through a failure to realize the shadow of the past, which the Christian Church has thrown over the Jew and his outlook.

We must recognise that more is called for here than merely a frank recognition of past guilt—all too often it is vitiated by a "Yes . . . but . . ." Sin injures both the sinner and the one sinned against, and the sinner has no right to plead the short-comings of the one he has injured in justification or palliation of his acts, especially if he is the main cause of those short-comings.

Book after book has been written about certain aspects of Jewish national character; in most cases they generalize quite unjustifiably, and normally fail to realize the inevitable effects of human sin. From the time of Constantine the Great (324-337) the Jew has been consistently treated by Christians and Muslims alike as a second-rate citizen, even though there might be temporary exceptions. Sometimes the discriminations were absurd, sometimes degrading. At regular intervals

[2] Published in *New Directions in Faith and Order: Bristol* 1967.

along this path he was robbed, or murdered, or driven out to find a home, he knew not where. At rare intervals it seemed as though he had found a home, peace, security—in Egypt in the 13th Century, in Spain, in Safed in the 16th century, in Poland—but in every case his hopes were dashed to the ground. When, finally, last century, it seemed that Emancipation had brought day at last, the sun set red behind the smoke from the furnaces of the extermination camps. Even in America, in spite of his prosperity—yet 16% of the community lives under the official poverty line—the Jew fears antisemitism and is confounded by the growing hatred shown him by the blacks, even though the Jewish community has always been a protagonist of racial equality.

Just as the deprived child may later become the demanding adolescent, so the Christian may be seriously embarrassed by the claims the Jew makes upon him, claims in which money play little or no part.

The second largest Jewish community in the world lives in the U.S.S.R. Estimates of its number vary between two and a half and three and a half million; the most recent census figures favour the lower estimate, but we must not forget that it is not an advantage to proclaim oneself a Jew in Russia, and the authorities have their own reasons for keeping the figure low. Sometimes higher figures are suggested but they are not likely to be correct, for the chief centres of Jewish population were overrun by the Germans during the last war. We need not doubt that the early communist leaders were sincere in their rejection of antisemitism, but for all that it has been a power, sometimes underground, sometimes openly, in Russia ever since the death of Lenin; today life has become intolerable for many Jews there. In the West many Jews find it hard to understand why so few Christians support them in their anti-Russian demonstrations. It might be harder still to explain why down the decades we have acquiesced in Russia's bitterly anti-religious policy, and indeed in that of the communist countries generally. Communist food, oil, mechanical products and culture have been more important to the Gentile, even to many Gentile Christians, than the fate of those who have had to suffer for their faith, Jews and Muslims as well as Christians. So we find it hard to be stirred by the plight of those prepared to risk prison and labour camp for the slight hope of escaping from the Soviet "paradise".

The Jewish partners in a dialogue group in New York were scandalized, when their Christian partners and indeed the Christian churches generally, did not stand openly and immediately on the Jewish side, when the Six-Day War broke out in 1967. In part, but only in part, this was due to the organizational red-tape that besets probably every larger denomination. The main reason was that very few Christians share the Jewish concept of the State of Israel as a categorical imperative, a must of human history, the only way of removing a sore that has troubled Western and Near-Eastern life for fifteen centuries. Those who do so are often moved more by their interpretation of prophecy than by human considerations.

The trouble is that the Christian, where he cannot wash his hands of the whole question, would like to sit above these problems, thinking out just and equitable solutions. He does not like it when the Jew tells him that, while he is not asking him to be partisan and unjust, he must not forget that he has played a fateful and even major part in the creation of the present situation.

The Christian must not shut his ears to the plea of the Palestinian Arab that he has been wronged, even if he is partly to blame for the situation in which he finds himself. Even less may he shut his eyes to the plight of the Palestinian refugees, even if for political reasons it has been made far worse than it need have been. But he is under compulsion to try and understand the Jewish position and outlook in penitent love. When there is loving understanding on the Christian side, the Jew may learn to understand the Arab standpoint more readily.

Above all he must be willing to simplify the situation by ceasing to insist on Christian holy places. With few exceptions the Arab record on holy places in more recent years calls for no criticism—it is a pity that they did not have a better record with the West Wall[3]—and the Jewish record is even better, so the Christian has no need to stake his claims.

It could be that the contribution of the Christian churches may have to be a massive donation towards the cost of restoring normality not as a gesture of reparation, but as a sincere effort to undo some of the effects of its wrong-doing in years gone by. It is all too little realized, except by experts,

[3] The Jewish name for the "Wailing Wall."

that the Crusades, with their massacres of Muslims as well as of Jews, radically changed the relationship between Muslims and Christians in the Near East. In any case the Jew expects Christian recognition that it is involved in these problems through the wrongs of the past.

Chapter XII

PROPHECY

THE only reason for this chapter is that, ever since the days of the Primitive Church, it has been taken for granted by so many that the bridge between Christians and Jews is supplied by Old Testament prophecy. So much is this the case that many Jews take it for granted as well and feel they have disposed of Christ by rejecting Christian prophetic interpretation. In modern dialogue it plays virtually no part.

We should remember that just as the modern liberal Christian seldom has any interest in prophecy as foretelling, so it is too with the liberal Jew. Obviously the non-religious Jew has even less interest in it, unless indeed it is as a sort of intellectual game. So for a large section of our contacts the subject is virtually meaningless.

The position of the Orthodox Jew is not very different, though here the reason is another. In the first place Orthodox interest, as we have seen earlier, is centred on the Torah. It is there that the problems created by the Messianic claims of Jesus and their interpretation by the Church are centred. There is a deeper and more practical reason as well.

Even in Justin's *Dialogue with Trypho,* based mainly on the understanding of prophecy, though it is a genuine dialogue reported only from the Christian side, we have the impression that Trypho is being polite, that he is listening to what Justin has to say—Justin does most of the talking—so that he may the more effectively counter Christian arguments in the future. But for all that Trypho was a willing participant.

It was not always the Christian who emerged the victor in such a dialogue, and conversions to Judaism were not unknown. When Christianity had the power of the state behind it, the winning of a Christian to Judaism became a criminal offence, finally punishable by death for the converter and converted. Clearly then discussion on prophecy held few attractions to the Jew.

Later it became a new distraction at the court of a great

landed ruler or high ecclesiastic to demand a debate between a Christian, normally a Dominican friar, and a representative of the local Jewish community, normally its rabbi. The conditions were that the loser should accept the religion of the conqueror or pay for his obstinacy with his life. Since the local magnate acted as judge, the result was a foregone conclusion, and the rabbi considered himself fortunate, if he escaped with banishment from the realm.

There were certain obvious consequences. The firmly rooted tendency to depreciate the Prophets in the interest of Torah was increased to the point where knowledge of the prophetic books might be restricted to the passages read in the regular Synagogue lectionary (the Haphtorah). Even more important was the abandonment of traditional interpretations in favour of those that would give no handle to a Christian adversary, the most obvious case of this being the prophecy of the Suffering Servant in Isa. 53, cf. Ch.VI.

The position may well be illustrated by a personal experience. I was introduced by a Hebrew Christian to an Orthodox rabbi famous for his loyalty to the Torah, who was also liberal enough to recognize the reality of Christian living. After some minutes of conversation, the one responsible for the introduction raised the question of Messianic prophecy. The rabbi looked me in the eyes and said, "You know that I know all the answers to the traditional Christian arguments." I could only answer, "Of course you do, and I have not come here to argue about Messianic prophecy. I would not dare to talk about it, unless you wish me to".

It could be argued that Christian exposition of prophecy by word of mouth or in print has been the means of convincing many Jews of the validity of the claims of Jesus Christ. This is undoubtedly true, not merely for the past but also today, but we tend to put the wrong interpretation on the fact. In spite of the sins and shortcomings of the Church, the attractiveness of Jesus has repeatedly been sensed by the individual Jew, especially when it has been mediated through Christian love. Once the emotions have been captured, the intellect is ready to be convinced. There are, however, very few who are prepared to alter the whole tenor of their life, to abandon their old allegiances and friends purely on intellectual grounds. Indeed, more often than not, men resent efforts to drive them logically to a change of their basic position. If any proof of this is needed, one should think only of cigarette smoking. The majority of the adult population is now convinced that it seriously increases the risk of lung cancer, but this has had very little effect on the total amount smoked. There is an enormous controversial literature of Rome versus Protestantism, of Episcopalianism versus Presbyterianism, of Paedobaptism versus Believer's Baptism, of Calvinism versus Arminianism, etc. but few there are that have been convinced by it. So while the evidence of prophecy may weigh with the influenced individual, it is not likely to play much part in intelligent dialogue between a Jew and a Christian.

There is a further point to be taken into consideration. Until a little more than a century ago, Jew, Christian and Muslim alike looked on their sacred books largely as depositories of proof texts, which could be interpreted without reference to their context, an attitude which is far from being dead even today. Increasingly, however, the educated man realizes that the context must be taken into consideration in the use and interpretation of a text.

It is still very widely assumed that the New Testament use of the Old conformed to the traditional practice, but C. H. Dodd in, *According to the Scriptures* has demonstrated that when the New Testament is quoting the Old, the verse used is normally a reference to a whole passage. If this is grasped, our whole attitude towards prophecy is likely to be changed.

Jew and Christian alike agree that the Old Testament is an incomplete book. For the traditional Jew the completion is to be found in the standard rabbinic works, which enjoy general acceptance, and in their application to present conditions. The Liberal Jew will use the general ethical and philosophical outlook of modern man for the purpose. The Christian sees all the lines of Old Testament thought coming to focus in Jesus Christ in the New Testament, though, according to his churchmanship, he is likely to appeal to the Church Fathers or outstanding theologians for a definitive interpretation.

Any Biblical and theological presentation of Jesus to a Jew is bound to attempt to show that He is the summing up of the revelation of God and that all truth meets in Him. Inevitably and rightly the Christian will increasingly point to Jesus as the fulfilment of the whole tenor of prophecy, not merely of this or that text.[1] But even such a use of prophecy will not convince the Jew, unless the heart has first been engaged.

[1] My treatment of the subject under the title *Christ the Corner Stone* should appear in 1972.

BIBLIOGRAPHY

The expert or near-expert on Judaism requires neither this book nor guidance on further reading. The following list, therefore omits those works, whose appeal is mainly to experts. Books published only in America are, for practical reasons, normally not mentioned. Many are out of print but should be available in a good library. Those mentioned in foot-notes have normally not been repeated here.

GENERAL

R. J. Zwi Werblowsky & G. Wigoder, *The Encyclopedia of the Jewish Religion*. This will probably be found the most useful of the one-volume encyclopedias.

J. Jocz, *The Jewish People and Jesus Christ* (S.P.C.K.) This offers a mine of information on the main themes of this book

P. Schneider, *Sweeter than Honey* (S.C.M.). An eirenic introduction for the Christian to Judaism.

The Jewish Year Book (Jewish Chronicle). There is much miscellaneous information to be found here.

THE SYNAGOGUE AND ITS SERVICES

Authorised Daily Prayer Book. The most useful edition for the non-Jew is that with Commentary by J. H. Hertz (Shapiro Vallentine).

The Passover Haggadah. There are many editions available.

W. W. Simpson, *Jewish Prayer and Worship* (S.C.M.) A simple and understanding introduction by a Christian.

W. O. E. Oesterly & G. H. Box, *The Religion and Worship of the Synagogue* (Pitman). For long the standard work in English.

I. Levy, *The Synagogue, Its History and Function* (Vallentine Mitchell). Except for the effort to find a pre-exilic origin for the Synagogue an excellent work.

HISTORY OF THE JEWS AND ANTISEMITISM

C. Roth, *A Short History of the Jewish People* (East & West Library). The standard one-volume work in English.

J. Parkes, *A History of the Jewish People* (Weidenfeld & Nicolson and Pelican Books). A survey by a master.

J. Parkes, *The Conflict of the Church and the Synagogue* (Soncino and Meridian Books). The standard work on the growth of anti-Judaism in the first eight centuries.

J. Parkes, *Antisemitism* (Vallentine Mitchell and Pelican Books). Deals with modern period.

N. Cohn, *Warrant for Genocide* (Eyre & Spottiswoode and Pelican Books). A history of *The Protocols of the Elders of Zion*.

H. D. Leuner, *When Compassion was a Crime* (Wolff). German Christian reactions against Nazi persecution of the Jews.

JUDAISM

A. Cohen, *Everyman's Talmud* (Dent). An excellent introduction to the Talmud and its contents.

M. Waxman, *Judaism, Religion and Ethics* (Yoseloff). Not too technical but gives details often found only in larger works.

I. Epstein, *Judaism* (Pelican Books). A very compact treatment.

S. S. Cohon, *Judaism, A Way of Life* (Schocken). A simpler treatment, written with Christian readers in mind.

M. Friedlander, *The Jewish Religion* (Shapiro Vallentine). Thorough orthodoxy finds its expression!

Leo Baeck, *The Essence of Judaism* (Macmillan). Generally regarded as a classic exposition of the liberal outlook.

I. I. Mattuck, *The Essentials of Liberal Judaism* (Routledge). Simpler and shorter.

M. Simon, *Jewish Religious Conflicts* (Hutchinson). By concentrating on the conflicts and splits within Judaism its inner nature is drawn out.

ANTHOLOGIES

C. G. Montefiore & H. Loewe, *A Rabbinic Anthology* (Macmillan & Meridian Books). The best anthology of rabbinic teaching down to A.D. 250.

A. Hertzberg, *Judaism* (Prentice-Hall). This gives a wide and well ordered selection, old and new.

J. H. Hertz, *A Book of Jewish Thoughts* (Oxford). The Jewish reader is mainly in mind; it was first compiled for Jewish service men.

ZIONISM AND THE STATE OF ISRAEL

Out of a plethora of works I menton only three:

Ch. Weizmann, *Trial and Error* (East & West Library).

C. Sykes, *Crossroads to Israel* (Collins and Nel Mentor).

A. J. Heschel, *Israel, An Echo of Eternity* (Noonday Press). The effect of Israel on a great liberal scholar.

Printed by
The Good News Press
Ongar (2106) Essex